The Official Guide to PTE Academic

for Test Takers

David Hill & Simon Cotterill

NEW EDITION

Contents

How to use the Official Guide	4
About PTE Academic	6
Getting to know the test	8
Preparing for your test	10
On test day	13
Score reports	15

Part 1

Speaking and writing — 19

Speaking — 20
- Personal introduction — 23
- Read aloud — 25
- Repeat sentence — 29
- Describe image — 33
- Re-tell lecture — 37
- Answer short question — 41
- Building confidence: speaking — 45

Writing — 48
- Summarize written text — 51
- Write essay — 55
- Building confidence: writing — 59

Part 2

Reading — 62
- Fill in the blanks: reading and writing — 65
- Multiple-choice: Choose multiple answers — 69
- Re-order paragraphs — 73
- Fill in the blanks: reading — 77
- Multiple-choice: Choose single answer — 81
- Building confidence: reading — 85

Part 3

Listening — 88
- Summarize spoken text — 91
- Multiple-choice: Choose multiple answers — 95
- Fill in the blanks: listening and writing — 99
- Highlight correct summary — 103
- Multiple-choice: Choose single answer — 107
- Select missing word — 111
- Highlight incorrect words — 115
- Write from dictation — 119
- Building confidence: listening — 123

Glossary — 126

How to Use the Official Guide

❯ Introduction

The Official Guide to PTE Academic, provides a complete overview of the test structure. It includes everything you need to know in order to become familiar with the task types, as well as guidance on managing a computer-based test and preparation strategies. *The Official Guide* and its support resources can also help you to practice real-world English skills in order to prepare for the PTE Academic test. It is an excellent starting point for evaluating your reading, writing, speaking and listening skills, and planning your test preparation.

❯ Resources

The Official Guide is divided into 3 main Resources:

The Official Guide Book

Online Practice Bank

Online Resources

❯ The Book

The *Official Guide to PTE Academic*:

- is suitable for anyone who wants to become familiar with the test;
- is designed to be used as a self-study tool, in addition to other preparation courseware or as part of classroom preparation;
- includes paper-based study and practice (with practice exercises included in the book and downloadable resources for printing) as well as online practice of all the tasks types;
- is a useful resource to help test takers plan their study and preparation for the test;
- is divided into clear sections to make information easy to find.

Information about PTE Academic

The pages at the front of the book give useful information on the test and what to expect, such as:

- guidance on how to prepare for your test
- information on how PTE A is scored and score reports
- complete overview of the test structure and detailed information on each Section

Skill Building pages

These can be found at the end of each the speaking, writing, reading and listening task type sections and provide:

- guidance on how to build different skills
- checklists for checking skill development
- tips for building test confidence

Task type pages

These pages give a detailed walkthrough of each task type and what is expected in the test. They also offer:

- **in depth** and **fast track** signposting to help you study in detail or prepare for your test quickly
- strategies for applying before and during the test
- suggestions for online resources and practice for each task type
- reminders to watch the videos

Glossary

This handy section details useful words and phrases related to PTE Academic and their meanings.

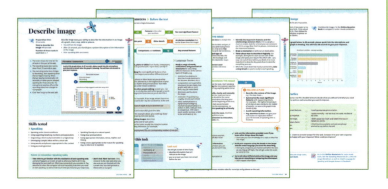

❯ The Online Resources

You can access these resources using the code for the **Pearson English Portal** printed in the front of your book.

Resource	Description	How to use it
General	**Answer keys** for all tasks in the book, including model answers for speaking and writing tasks	Check your answers and see model responses to tasks.
	Academic Collocations List	Use this list to improve your academic vocabulary.
	***Am I ready?* checklist**	You can use this before you start studying to identify areas for improvement. Use it during your preparation for the test to measure your skill progress.
Audio	**Audio tracks** for both practice tasks in the book, as well as model answers	Use these while practising the tasks in the book.
	Speaking Sample Answer audio tracks	Use these with the speaking sample answer and feedback downloadable material.
Video	**20 Videos**, focusing on the common mistakes people make when approaching each task type.	Watch the videos after studying the task type information in the *Official Guide*.
Speaking	**Worksheets for Speaking tasks:** Personal Introduction Read aloud Repeat sentence Describe image Re-tell lecture	Choose which worksheets you want to do in order to improve specific speaking skills or practice a particular task type in more detail. The sample answers and feedback will give you some examples of typical test taker responses at different levels. Use these to reflect on your own speaking practice and reflect on where you can improve.
	Speaking Sample Answers and Feedback Personal Introduction Describe image Repeat sentence Re-tell lecture Summarize spoken text	
	Useful Language for Speaking	This resource can help you to develop language skills for speaking.
Writing	**Worksheets for Writing tasks:** Write essay Summarize written text	Choose which worksheets you want to do in order to improve specific writing skills or practice a particular task type in more detail. The sample answers and expert feedback will give you some examples of typical written test taker responses. Compare them to your own responses and reflect on where you can improve.
	Written Sample Answers and Feedback Write essay Summarize written text	
	How to Structure Academic Writing: essays **How to Structure Academic Writing: summarising texts**	Use these resources if you want to improve your writing skills for academic purposes.
	Useful Language for Writing	This resource can help you to develop language skills for writing.
General Skill Development	**How to Improve Speaking Skills** **How to Improve Writing Skills** **How to Improve Listening Skills** **How to Improve Reading Skills**	General information divided by speaking, writing, listening and reading. Includes some general guidance and some specific tips on how to improve your communicative skills for PTE Academic.
Online Practice Bank	**300 PTE Academic practice questions,** covering all 20 scored task types and Personal introduction	Use the bank to: • Practise the tasks that are included the book online, timed as you do them in the test • Listen to sample answers for speaking and writing tasks after you have given your responses and compare them to your own • Get additional tips per task type

HOW TO USE THE OFFICIAL GUIDE | **5**

About PTE Academic

About the test

Pearson Test of English Academic (or PTE Academic) is a computer-based English proficiency test, which is widely recognised around the world as an accurate and reliable measure of English skills. Academic institutions, professional organisations and government bodies in many countries use PTE Academic results to make decisions on student admissions and visa applications. With approved test centres in over 50 countries and regions of the world, the test is widely recognised for its straightforward registration process and quick delivery of scores.

PTE Academic is an unbiased, authentic, and entirely digital test which uses artificial intelligence to score responses in an impartial way. Its integrated skills tasks mean that you must combine your language skills (reading and writing or listening and speaking) in a variety of ways. This is at the same time as performing real-life tasks such as summarising an authentic text or retelling information from a lecture. The result is a comprehensive assessment of your proficiency in English. As you will need to perform authentic academic tasks, preparing for the PTE Academic, also means preparing to successfully use English in real-life academic situations.

The test's detailed Score Report provides information that helps you clearly identify specific areas for improvement. Scores are reported according to the **Global Scale of English** (GSE), which is aligned to the **Common European Framework of Reference** (CEFR).

How the test works

PTE Academic can be taken at any of the authorised test centres around the world. The whole test lasts approximately three hours. The test has three parts: Speaking and Writing, Reading, and Listening. There are 20 different types of scored tasks in the test and one more that is not scored. However, this doesn't mean that there are only 20 questions. You will complete each task type a number of times. The task types all have names (e.g. *Re-tell Lecture, Repeat sentence,* etc.) which makes it easier to identify each one and remember what you need to do.

Task types focus on English as it is used in real-life academic situations. They feature authentic texts: audio and video recordings from academic disciplines in Arts, Humanities, Sciences and Social Sciences. Each task is based on a topic (e.g. the climate change or marketing strategies) and although you do not need detailed knowledge of the topics to complete the tasks, you will need sufficient language skills to be able to analyse the information and respond successfully.

In everyday life, we don't use language skills (such as reading and listening) in isolation. So, PTE Academic uses integrated skills tasks (i.e. tasks that require you to use multiple skills at once) in a similar way that these skills are used in real life. For example, *Summarize written text* involves reading an academic text and writing a summary of it. This is something students regularly do in higher education or apply as a skill in professional life.

All tasks are scored using PTE Academic's automated scoring system. Test results are usually delivered within just a couple of days of taking the test. And the use of artificial intelligence means that scores are awarded reliably by a computer without risk of human error or bias. The scoring system, which has been developed based on the responses of thousands of test takers, produces accurate scores, is consistent, objective, and fair.

The test taking process

Every test taker will need to give some consideration to the following.

1 Is PTE Academic right for you?

Before taking PTE Academic, decide if it is the right test for you. Check whether PTE Academic is accepted by the institution(s) you are applying to. Find out at **www.pearsonpte.com** or contact the institution directly.

2 Identify when you need to take the test

If you are using your PTE score for a specific purpose, find out the application deadlines for your chosen institution(s) and work out exactly how much time you have to prepare.

3 Book your test

Book your test at an approved centre by creating a PTE Academic account online at **www.pearsonpte.com**. You can book a test for any day of the week, and last-minute bookings with 24 hours' notice are sometimes possible.

4 Evaluate your goals

Before you start preparing:
1. Identify your target score.
2. Evaluate your proficiency level in English and where you could improve.
3. Evaluate how familiar you are with the test and use the *Official Guide* to help you.

5 Decide how you will prepare

If you have a longer period to prepare for the test, look for the *In depth* study logo throughout the *Official Guide*.

Plan to use as many of the **Online Resources** as you can, including the **Online Question Bank** to help you improve your skills..

If you have a limited amount of time to prepare for the test, look for the *Fast track* logo throughout the *Official Guide* to find the main information. Focus on familiarising yourself with the task types by using the **Online Question Bank** and watching the **Common mistakes** videos. Use the **Online Resources** to focus on any areas you find challenging.

6 Check if you are ready

Check if you are ready for the test by using the *Am I ready checklist?* in the **Online Resources** or by taking a **Scored Practice Test** online. (go to **www.pearsonpte.com** for more information).

7 Take the test

The test lasts approximately three hours. You should arrive at the test centre at least 30 minutes before the test starts in order to complete security and sign-in procedures.

8 Wait for your results

After taking the test, you will be notified by email when your PTE Academic scores are available (typically within two working days). Using your account, you can view your scores and send them to institutions if you need to.

Getting to know the test

How the test is structured

PTE Academic consists of three main parts: Speaking and Writing, Reading, and Listening. The entire test takes approximately three hours to complete and is taken on a computer at an approved test centre. Questions are always randomly generated by the computer, which means that no two PTE Academic tests are the same. You will complete all scored 20 task types, but the number of times each one appears will vary between tests. For example, you might have to complete *Describe image* six times, but another test-taker may do it seven times. This means that timings will vary too. The computer creates the test in this way in order to rigorously assess a wide range of language skills.

Part 1: Speaking and writing

Part 1 takes **77–93 minutes to complete.** Although this part requires you to demonstrate your speaking and writing skills, some integrated tasks assess reading or listening skills, too.

Part 1 also assesses your ability to use six enabling skills: grammar, oral fluency, pronunciation, spelling, vocabulary and written discourse.

Part 1 is divided into **six sections, each with a separate time limit**. Sections 1 and 2 focus on speaking and Sections 3–6 on writing. There are **six different kinds of speaking task in** Sections 1 and 2, as well as **two different kinds of writing task** in sections 3–6.

- **Section 1** is an unscored task which requires you to start speaking, give a brief description of yourself and your goals, and allow the system to identify your voice. This task is a good opportunity to introduce yourself, relax, and get used to the equipment and the test environment.
- **Section 2** task types all require spoken responses. In this section you complete 35–42 tasks in total.
- In **Sections 3–6** you complete one writing task per section, four writing tasks in total. These individual tasks take longer to complete than those in Sections 1 and 2, and each task has its own strict time limit.

Part 2: Reading

Part 2 takes **32–41 minutes to complete.**

All tasks in Part 2 contribute to the reading score, and one task type (*Reading & writing: Fill in the blanks*) also contributes to the writing score.

There are **five task types**, which involve reading about a range of authentic academic topics, answering multiple-choice questions and completing texts by filling in gaps or re-ordering sentences.

There is **a single time limit** for completing this part of the test and you must complete **15–20 tasks** in total.

Part 3: Listening

Part 3 takes **45–57 minutes** and features a range of audio and video recordings. In each task, the **audio or video recording is only played once**.

Part 3 is divided into **two Sections which both focus on listening**. There is **one task type** in Section 1 and **six kinds of speaking task** in Section two. All tasks contribute to the listening score, while some also contribute to scores for reading and writing.

There are **two sections in Part 3.**

- In section 1 you complete 2–3 *Summarize spoken texts* tasks. These tasks assess listening and writing, as well as grammar, spelling and vocabulary.
- In section 2 you complete **15–22 tasks** in total.

Test overview

This table shows the test structure.

Parts of test	Section	Task type	Number of tasks in the test	Time allowed
Introduction				Not timed
Part 1: Speaking and writing	Section 1	Personal introduction	1	1 minute
	Section 2	Read aloud	6–7	30–35 minutes
		Repeat sentence	10–12	
		Describe image	6–7	
		Re-tell lecture	3–4	
		Answer short question	10–12	
	Sections 3–4	Summarize written text	2	20 minutes
	Section 5	Summarize written text or Write essay	1	10 or 20 minutes
	Section 6	Write essay	1	20 minutes
Part 2: Reading		Fill in the blanks: reading and writing	5–6	32–41 minutes
		Multiple-choice, choose multiple answers	2–3	
		Re-order paragraphs	2–3	
		Fill in the blanks: reading	4–5	
		Multiple-choice, choose single answer	2–3	
Part 3: Listening	Section 1	Summarize spoken text	2–3	20 or 30 minutes
	Section 2	Multiple-choice, choose multiple answers	2–3	23–28 minutes
		Fill in the blanks: listening	2–3	
		Highlight correct summary	2–3	
		Multiple-choice, choose single answer	2–3	
		Select missing word	2–3	
		Highlight incorrect words	2–3	
		Write from dictation	3–4	

Preparing for your test

Getting started | Depending on your needs, language level and familiarity with the test, preparing to take PTE Academic can include these things:

Deciding when to take the test

Start by deciding when you need to receive your results. If you'll be taking PTE Academic for a specific purpose, you should identify:

- any specific institution(s) you want to apply to;
- the target or minimum score you need;
- the application deadline(s) you need to meet.

Don't leave it too late to take the test. PTE Academic scores are typically delivered within two working days but you should plan the date carefully. At the same time, try to give yourself the maximum time possible to prepare for the test and focus on improving your academic skills in English.

Familiarising yourself with the test

This guide will allow you to build familiarity with the PTE Academic format and the test-taking experience. You may not perform as well as you can if you are surprised by something or if you don't know exactly what to do.

Understanding the demands of each task type

PTE Academic has 20 different task types. You need to use different skills to approach each one. Read the step-by-step explanation of each task type in the *Official Guide* and use the **Online Question Bank** to practise each task type.

- Get familiar with each task type, so you don't have to spend time during the test understanding what to do.
- Understand the skills you will be scored on for each task type.
- Prepare yourself for what you will see on screen. Knowing in advance exactly where to find different functions (e.g. play button, time counter and recording status) can save you time during the test, as well as improve your confidence.

Evaluating your English proficiency

Before deciding on the best way to study for PTE Academic, you need to identify your main strengths and weaknesses in English and academic skills. First, use these diagrams to consider the different sub-skills involved in using English effectively in academic contexts.

Understanding academic English

- READING ACADEMIC TEXTS
  - Identifying a writer/speaker's attitude
  - Distinguishing the most important information in a text/lecture
  - Thinking critically about information
  - Working out the meaning of unfamiliar vocabulary
- UNDERSTANDING LECTURES AND CONVERSATIONS

Using English in academic contexts

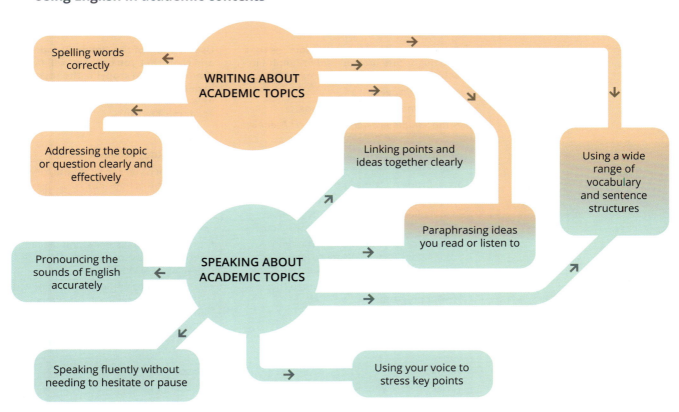

- WRITING ABOUT ACADEMIC TOPICS
  - Spelling words correctly
  - Addressing the topic or question clearly and effectively
  - Linking points and ideas together clearly
  - Paraphrasing ideas you read or listen to
  - Using a wide range of vocabulary and sentence structures
- SPEAKING ABOUT ACADEMIC TOPICS
  - Pronouncing the sounds of English accurately
  - Speaking fluently without needing to hesitate or pause
  - Using your voice to stress key points

PREPARING FOR YOUR TEST

Deciding how to prepare

PTE Academic is used for a range of purposes, by a wide variety of test takers. For this reason, preparation time can vary a lot between test takers. Some may prepare for their test quickly in a short period of time, while others may need to improve their level of proficiency and take a longer route to preparing for their test. The *Official Guide* offers advice on how to approach the test, whatever your situation.

 If you have a reduced amount of time to prepare for your test, look for the *fast track* **preparation** symbol, for concise guidance and the main information you need to know.

 If you have longer to prepare, follow the *in depth* **study** symbol for advice on how to study for the test in more detail.

Following a study plan

However long you have to prepare for the test, it is important to create a study plan to make sure you cover everything you need. See the chart below for suggested steps for creating a *fast track* or an *in depth* study plan.

	Fast track preparation	In depth study
Step 1	Check the test date and count how many weeks you have.	Check the test date and count how many weeks you have.
Step 2	**Identify your strengths and areas for improvement** • Complete a **Scored Practice Test**. • Use the ***Effective Skills Checklists*** in this guide, to identify strong and weak points (pages 46, 60, 86 and 124). • With the task types in mind, make a list of the specific tasks you want to get more familiar with.	**Identify your strengths and areas for improvement** • Complete the ***Am I ready?* Checklist** • Use the ***Effective Skills Checklists*** in this guide, to identify strong and weak points (pages 46, 60, 86 and 124). • Make a list of the areas where you want to improve, focusing both on task types and improving your overall English skills.
Step 3	**Pick out the *Official Guide* resources that you might find most useful or helpful in achieving your goals.** These might include: • the *Worksheets* • the *Common mistakes* videos • the *Sample Answers and Expert Feedback*	**Use as many of the Online Resources and tools that you can.** You will find them helpful in studying the task types in detail and practising with them, as well as improving your skills in academic English.
Step 4	**Create a study schedule** Identify when you can study and for how long. Divide this time into: • active practice of the specific skills you identified as needing improvement in Step 2 by using targeted online resources • active practice of the task types you identified as needing improvement in Step 2 using the **Online Question Bank** • taking **Scored Practice Tests** to check your progress.	**Create a study schedule** Identify when you can study and for how long. Divide this time into: • practising your speaking and writing as much as possible to build your skills and confidence; • practising your listening and reading through exposure to academic texts and audio or video • active practice of the specific skills you identified as needing improvement in Step 2 • active practice of all twenty task types using the **Online Question Bank**.
Step 5	**Re-assessing** A week before your test: • take a **Scored Practice Test**. • complete the ***Am I ready?* Checklist**. Are there any areas you still need to work on?	**Re-assessing** Before your test: • take **Scored Practice Tests**. • complete the ***Am I ready?* Checklist**. Are there any areas you still need to work on?

On test day

Things to do before going to the test centre

- Read your confirmation email carefully.
- Pack the correct ID as requested by the test centre (usually your passport). The details on your ID must match those entered when booking the test. Without the correct ID, you cannot take the test.
- Check the exact test centre address.
- Plan your journey carefully.
- Make sure you leave enough time for potential delays, such as rush hour traffic.
- Arrive at least 30 minutes before your test start time for security and sign-in procedures. If you are late, you won't be allowed to take the test.

Arriving at the test centre

When you arrive at the test centre, you will be given instructions to follow. You must do what the test centre staff ask you as they need to check who you are carefully for security.

1 Show your ID.

2 Read the *PTE Academic Test Taker Rules Agreement*, which details what you must and mustn't do during the test. Ask a member of staff if there is anything you don't understand.

3 Sign in digitally to accept the agreement. Once you have signed the agreement, you agree to abide by the terms of the test. Failing to follow these terms and instructions may jeopardise your test.

4 Scan your palm and have your photograph taken. These security measures validate your identity and the authenticity of the test.

5 You will be asked to leave all personal items in a locker, including any mobile devices, which should be switched off. Store all personal items in the locker provided.

The following items are **not** allowed in the test room:
- phones
- electronic devices
- digital watches
- food and drink of any kind
- large items of jewellery (thicker than ¼ inch/ ½ cm)
- wallets or purses
- hats
- coats
- books, notes or paper
- smoking
- talking to other test takers

6 You will receive a pen and erasable booklet which you can use to make notes during the test if you wish.

Do not write on the erasable booklet until the test begins. You can use both sides of the erasable booklet to write on. If you need more pages during the test, the administrator can give you a new one.

Go!

Starting your test

- Once it is time to start your test, the test administrator will take you into the test room and give you a seat.
- The test administrator will sign you into your computer.
- Each computer booth has a computer, a keyboard and a set of headphones with a microphone.
- The screen will guide you through the steps you need to follow in order to make sure everything is working correctly.
- If there are any issues, raise your hand and inform the test administrator.

During your test

- During speaking tasks, you speak into the microphone and your responses will be recorded. When speaking, do not raise your voice. Speak at a normal, conversational level.
- You will not be able to re-record your responses. You only get one chance each time.
- There will be other test takers in the room, and they may be speaking at the same time as you. Try to concentrate on your own test and what you need to do. Keep your headset on during the entire test.
- During writing tasks, type your answers on the keyboard.
- You can use any form of English (e.g. American, British, etc.) but you must be consistent within responses.
- If you do not complete tasks within the time limits, the computer will automatically move you on to the next task.
- You cannot go back to change responses.
- If you have problems during the test, raise your hand and wait for the test administrator to come and help. Do not stand up or talk to the administrator or anyone else.
- When you finish, click on the **End Test button**. Raise your hand to let the administrator know you have finished.

Taking a break

- You can choose to take a ten-minute break after Part 2 of the test.
  - Follow the instructions on the screen.
  - You must inform the test administrator that you are taking a break or the timer may keep running, leaving you with less time to complete the test.
  - You must leave the room when taking a break.
  - You must return to the computer within ten minutes.
  - If you take too long, you will lose time from the next section.
  - You will not get extra time if you do not take the break.
- If you need a break, raise your hand to speak to the test administrator. The test clock will not stop during this break.
- During a break you cannot go to your locker.
- You must repeat the sign-in procedures to re-enter the test room.

Test day Dos and Don'ts

Do
✔ plan your journey before leaving the house.
✔ arrive at least 30 minutes before your test start time, for security and sign-in procedures.
✔ follow the instructions you see on the screen for checking equipment, such as the headphones and microphone.
✔ use your microphone to make a test recording, as instructed, and play it back to check your voice is being captured correctly.
✔ raise your hand to speak to the test administrator if you need a break or there is a problem. Test administrators are trained to help you.
✔ practise relaxation and/or concentration techniques in the time leading up to the test, if you are nervous or are distracted by others speaking.

Don't
✘ forget to take the correct ID (usually a passport) with you. This must match the ID you used to book the test.
✘ speak too loudly, or quietly, into the microphone, as this can prevent it capturing your voice properly, which could reduce your speaking score.
✘ talk to or distract other test takers, or speak to the test administrator. If you need a test administrator, raise your hand clearly and wait.
✘ allow yourself to be distracted by other test takers. You will be able to hear them doing their speaking tasks. Make an effort to block them out. Their tasks will be different from yours, so there is no benefit in listening to them.

Score reports

After the test

Everyone who takes PTE Academic receives a Score Report, which provides an overall score and individual scores for listening, reading, speaking and writing, as well as grammar, oral fluency, pronunciation, spelling, vocabulary and written discourse. These scores are reported on a scale of 10–90 points, which aligns with the **Global Scale of English** (GSE).

The chart below shows how the PTE Academic scoring scale of 10-90 reflects levels on the GSE scale.

GSE (PTE A)	10	20	30	40	50	60	70	80	90
CEFR	<A1	A1	A2	+	B1	+	B2 +	C1	C2

PTE Academic is scored using automated scoring. The automated scoring system is based on complex computer algorithms that were programmed using responses from more than 10,000 test takers from over 20 countries, who spoke more than 90 different first languages. The spoken and written responses of these test takers were rated by a large team of expert human markers who trained the automated scoring system to give more analytical and objective results than is possible for individuals. Unlike human judgement, which can be influenced by a variety of factors, (e.g. preferences of certain types of pronunciation or accent) the automated scoring system is impartial and unbiased.

Scoring requirements

Each institution or government body has its own set of requirements for PTE Academic scores needed to gain entry to academic courses or obtain visas. Higher-education institutions may require an overall score between 42 and 73 for direct entry to undergraduate or postgraduate degree courses, while overall scores of between 30 and 41 are often enough to join English courses that prepare students for higher education. Some institutions also require a minimum score in a specific skill, such as writing.

PTE Academic score requirements for work visas can vary widely, from 30–79 points, according to the type of visa. It is important to check the exact score requirements of the institution you are applying to regularly, as requirements can change over time.

Accessing your Score Report

You will typically be able to access your Score Reports within two working days. When the results are ready, you will receive an email at the address you provided during registration online. This email contains details of how to access your Score Report.

- Login to your account at **www.pearsonpte.com** to access your Score Report.
- Your Score Report will be issued to you in PDF format.
- Your Score Report is valid for two years from the date you take the test.
- Institutions will be able to verify your Score Report through an electronic verification platform.
- You will only be accepted by an institution after your Score Report is verified.
- To access your results, institutions will use the Score Report Code on your Score Report.

SCORE REPORTS

Score Reports

1. **Personal details:** The personal information supplied when booking the test.
2. **Test details:** Information about where and when the test was taken.
3. **Overall score:** The overall score is based on your performance for all tasks.
4. **Communicative skills scores:** Your score report will contain separate scores for the four communicative skills – listening, reading, speaking and writing. Each section of PTE Academic is designed to test your ability with a different communicative skill. However, these skills are often tested across sections. For example, *Summarize written text* tasks contribute to your scores for both reading and writing (as well as to your overall score).
5. **Enabling skills scores:** There are six enabling skills scores that you are also tested on. These enabling skills are grammar, oral fluency, pronunciation, spelling, vocabulary and written discourse.

Enabling skills are tested throughout PTE Academic and also contribute to your overall score. For example, *Write essay* tasks assess grammar, spelling, vocabulary and written discourse, while *Re-tell lecture* tasks test oral fluency and pronunciation.

Score Reports provide scores for each of these enabling skills in the same way as the communicative skills, on a scale of 10–90 points.

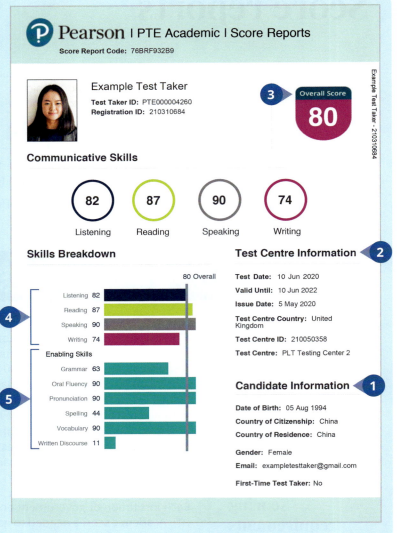

How tasks are scored

Not all tasks are scored in the same way. Scoring can be focused on your performance with a single communicative skill, or several communicative skills and sometimes, other enabling skills as well.

Correct or Incorrect

Some task types are scored as either **correct** or **incorrect.** For example, in *Multiple-choice, choose single answer* tasks, you receive **maximum** points for selecting the correct answer and **no points** for selecting an incorrect answer.

Partial credit

Some item types are scored as **correct, partially correct** or **incorrect.** For example, for *Multiple-choice, choose multiple answers* tasks, you receive maximum points for selecting only correct answers and partial credit for selecting one or two correct answers. Task types that require you to use your own words, such as *Re-tell lecture*, also award partial credit: you receive **maximum** points for re-telling all the main points of the lecture and **partial** credit for re-telling some of the main points.

Form

For *Summarize written text, Write essay* and *Summarize spoken text* tasks, scores are also awarded for **form**, based on whether a response is within the word limit for the task. For example, the length requirements for *Write essay* tasks is 200–300 words. You receive **maximum** points for form when you write responses that are 200–300 words long. **Partial credit** is awarded for writing 120–199 or 301–380 words. **No points** are awarded for form when responses are under 120 or over 380 words.

See the table on page 17 for an overview of scoring for each task type.

SCORE REPORTS

Task type	Skills assessed - Communicative skills	Enabling skills	Types of scoring	Partial credit criteria
Part 1: Speaking and writing				
Read aloud	Reading, speaking	Oral fluency, pronunciation	Partial credit	Number of words read aloud accurately/ Number of errors. Quality of pronunciation and oral fluency
Repeat sentence	Listening, speaking	Oral fluency, pronunciation	Partial credit	Number of words repeated accurately/ Number of errors. Quality of pronunciation and oral fluency
Describe image	Speaking	Oral fluency, pronunciation	Partial credit	Content of description: Number of key elements described. Quality of pronunciation and oral fluency
Re-tell lecture	Listening, speaking	Oral fluency, pronunciation	Partial credit	Content of Re-telling: Number of key points retold. Quality of pronunciation and oral fluency
Answer short question	Listening, speaking	Vocabulary	Correct/ Incorrect	
Summarize written text	Reading, writing	Grammar, vocabulary	Partial credit	Quality of summary: Number of relevant aspects mentioned. Form, accuracy of grammar, appropriateness of vocabulary
Write essay	Writing	Spelling, written discourse, grammar, vocabulary	Partial credit	Content: Extent prompt is dealt with, form, development, structure and coherence, accuracy of grammar, linguistic range, spelling
Part 2: Reading				
Reading & Writing: Fill in the blanks	Reading, writing		Partial credit	Number of correctly completed blanks
Multiple-choice, choose multiple answers	Reading		Partial credit	Points scored for selecting correct responses. Points deducted for selecting incorrect responses.
Re-order paragraphs	Reading		Partial credit	Correctly order, adjacent pairs of sentences.
Reading: Fill in the blanks	Reading		Partial credit	Number of correctly completed blanks
Multiple-choice, choose single answer	Reading		Correct/ Incorrect	
Part 3: Listening				
Summarize spoken text	Listening, writing	Spelling, grammar, vocabulary	Partial credit	Quality of summary: Number of relevant aspects mentioned. Form, accuracy of grammar, spelling, appropriateness of vocabulary
Multiple-choice, choose multiple answers	Listening		Partial credit	Points scored for selecting correct responses. Points deducted for selecting incorrect responses.
Fill in the blanks	Listening, writing		Partial credit	Number of words spelled correctly
Highlight correct summary	Listening, reading		Correct/ Incorrect	
Multiple-choice, choose single answer	Listening		Correct/ Incorrect	
Select missing word	Listening		Correct/ Incorrect	
Highlight incorrect word	Listening, reading		Partial credit	Points scored for selecting correct words. Points deducted for selecting incorrect word
Write from dictation	Listening, writing		Partial credit	Number of words spelled correctly

Enabling skills

Enabling skills are used in different tasks and for some tasks, contribute to overall scores. Scores for **enabling skills** are measured against specific criteria.

Enabling skill	Focus	Task
Grammar	Correct use of language at sentence level (e.g. word form and word order).	*Summarize written text, Write essay, Summarize spoken text*
Oral fluency	Smooth, effortless and natural-paced delivery.	*Read aloud, Repeat sentence, Describe image, Re-tell lecture*
Pronunciation	Production of speech sounds in a way that is easily understandable to most regular speakers of the language. Regional and national pronunciation variants are considered correct as long as they can be understood by a proficient speaker.	
Spelling	Writing correctly to English spelling rules; all national variations in spelling are considered correct.	*Write essay, Summarize spoken text*
Vocabulary	Use of appropriate words for precisely expressing meaning in written and spoken English; use of a wide range of language.	*Summarize written text, Write essay, Summarize spoken text, Answer short question*
Written discourse	Correctly written texts that effectively communicate ideas and meaning. Written responses show sufficient skills in the structure, coherence, logical development and the range of tools used for academic writing.	*Write essay*

Scoring examples

This is an example of how a *Write essay* task contributes to multiple scores.

If the response to a *Write essay* task meets the question requirements, it will receive a score for its content (how well the answer deals with the question), form (whether the answer is within the word limit), and the enabling skills tested. *Write essay* tasks contribute to your score for vocabulary, spelling, grammar and written discourse. Written discourse scores for *Write essay* are based on development, structure and coherence, as well as general linguistic range. Further details of these criteria can be found in the **Online Resources**.

The total task score will contribute to the communicative skills score (writing) and the overall score.

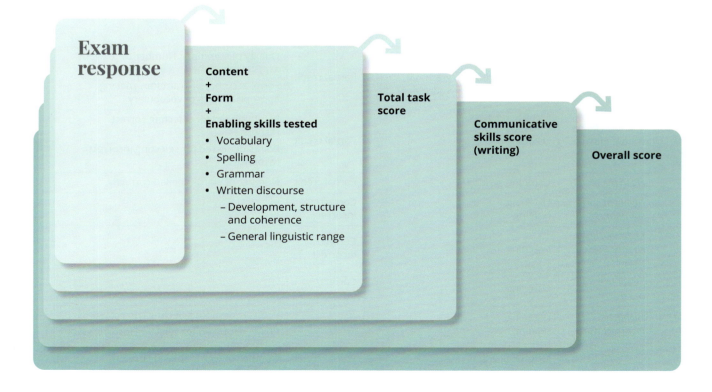

Part 1 | Speaking and writing

Overview

Part 1 of PTE Academic is focused on speaking and writing. This part tests your ability to produce spoken and written academic English.

Part 1 is **approximately 80–95 minutes** and is divided into **six Sections**. Section 1 and 2 are focused on speaking tasks, and sections 3–6 are focused on writing tasks.

There are **six task types** in sections 1 and 2 (the first section is unscored) and **two task types** in section 3–6. You will complete a **total of 40–48 tasks** in total across Part 1. Some integrated tasks will also assess reading and listening.

Part 1 (Speaking and writing)

	Task type	Number of tasks	Task description	Skills assessed	Text/Recording length	Time to answer
Speaking (Total time: 30–35 minutes)						
Section 1	Personal introduction	1	After reading the instructions, briefly introduce yourself.	Not scored	n/a	30 seconds
Section 2	Read aloud	6–7	A text appears on screen. Read the text aloud.	Reading and speaking	Up to 60 words	Varies
	Repeat sentence	10–12	After listening to a sentence, repeat it.	Listening and speaking	3–9 seconds	15 seconds
	Describe image	6–7	An image appears on screen. Describe it in detail.	Speaking	n/a	40 seconds
	Re-tell lecture	3–4	After listening to or watching a lecture, re-tell it in your own words.	Listening and speaking	Up to 90 seconds	40 seconds
	Answer short question	10–12	After listening to a question, answer it with a single word or short phrase.	Listening and speaking	3–9 seconds	10 seconds
Writing (Total time: 50–60 minutes)						
Sections 3–4	Summarize written text	2	After reading a passage, write a one-sentence summary.	Reading and writing	Text up to 300 words, answer up to 75 words	10 minutes each
Section 5	Summarize written text or Write essay	1	See above and below	Writing or Reading and writing	Word count depends on the task type	Timing depends on the task type
Section 6	Write essay	1	Write an essay of 200–300 words in response to a prompt.	Writing	Answer up to 300 words	20 minutes each

Part 1 | Speaking

What is assessed in the Speaking sections

PTE Academic assesses a range of speaking skills in this part of the test.

- Speaking for a purpose (e.g. repeating, informing and explaining)
- Reading a text aloud
- Summarising the main points of spoken and visual information
- Organising an oral presentation in a logical sequence
- Using vocabulary and expressions appropriate to the context
- Developing complex ideas within speech
- Using correct intonation, stress and pronunciation
- Speaking fluently and clearly

This part of the test assesses how well you can talk about academic topics. Tasks are based on a variety of texts, graphics, and audio and video recordings. For example, in *Read aloud* tasks, you read an academic text. For *Describe image* tasks, you talk about the main aspects of graphic material, such as a graph or a chart showing information about recent trends. For *Repeat sentence, Re-tell lecture,* and *Answer short question* tasks, you respond to audio or video input, such as an academic lecture.

You should speak fluently with good intonation, stress and pronunciation. PTE Academic recognises a range of regional and national varieties of English pronunciation, as long as you speak in a consistent way that is easily understandable to most English speakers.

Speaking skills

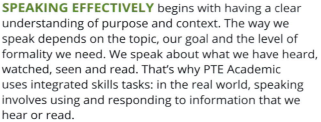

SPEAKING EFFECTIVELY begins with having a clear understanding of purpose and context. The way we speak depends on the topic, our goal and the level of formality we need. We speak about what we have heard, watched, seen and read. That's why PTE Academic uses integrated skills tasks: in the real world, speaking involves using and responding to information that we hear or read.

DEVELOPING SPEAKING SKILLS starts with using appropriate phrases and sentences to describe everyday topics. As our skills improve, we can give longer, more detailed responses to questions and descriptions about a wider range of topics. The most advanced speakers can talk fluently and easily about complex issues, using idiomatic and colloquial language with appropriate stress and intonation depending on the message they want to give.

What to expect in the speaking section

In PTE Academic, you speak into a microphone while looking at the screen. At the start of the test, check that the microphone is recording your voice correctly. After checking the recording volume, check that the volume of your voice is the same throughout the test. You can monitor the recording level on the screen.

There will probably be other test takers in the same room at the test centre. However, you should not speak too loudly into the microphone as a result. On the other hand, speaking too loudly can distort the recording, which can reduce your score. Speaking too quietly makes it hard for the computer to pick up what you are saying. Try to use your normal voice, as if you are talking to someone in front of you.

The speaking tasks feature authentic academic texts, graphics, and audio and video recordings. In tasks that involve listening, you will hear people with different accents and dialects. The recordings are extracts of longer authentic audio and video recordings, such as podcasts and academic lectures. This means that the speakers talk in a completely natural way and at a normal speed. This helps to prepare you for using English in real-world situations. You do not need to be familiar with the topic to complete the task successfully.

The total time limit for all speaking tasks is 30–35 minutes.

Speaking task types

At the start of Part 1, you will be asked to introduce yourself. Your response is not scored, but you can send it, along with your Score Report, to the institutions of your choice. It is also an additional security measure.

You will complete each of the five remaining task types a number of times (exact numbers vary between tests, but between three and twelve times per task type). Each task type has a different format:

- *Read aloud* tests your ability to read a short text with correct pronunciation and intonation.
- *Repeat sentence* requires you to understand, remember and repeat a short sentence exactly as you hear it, while using correct pronunciation.
- *Describe image* tests your ability to describe an image from an academic source.
- *Re-tell lecture* tests your ability to summarise the important information from a lecture.

Scoring of speaking tasks

Because PTE Academic is an integrated skills test, the speaking tasks in Part 1 contribute to the overall score, speaking score and also to the scores for reading, listening, oral fluency, pronunciation and vocabulary.

Task type	Overall score	Speaking score	Reading score	Listening score	Oral fluency score	Pronunciation score	Vocabulary score
Read aloud	✔	✔	✔		✔	✔	
Repeat sentence	✔	✔		✔	✔	✔	
Describe image	✔	✔			✔	✔	
Re-tell lecture	✔	✔		✔	✔	✔	
Answer short question	✔	✔		✔			✔

Managing the information on screen

At the start of the test, you will be able to read and listen to instructions that explain everything you need to do.

You will be shown how to check your microphone is in the correct position before the test begins. Make sure it stays in this position throughout the Speaking sections of the test.

1. Tasks begin with an instruction. After being presented with information such as a lecture for *Re-tell lecture*, a graphic for *Describe image*, or a written passage for *Read aloud* tasks, you record your spoken response into the microphone. The recording status box shows how much time you have to prepare before recording begins.

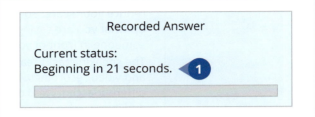

2. When recording begins, the recording status will change to 'Recording' and the bar will begin to fill, showing you how much time is left to give your answer.

3. During each task, you can see the timer. This tells you how much time remains for the task and for the section of the test.

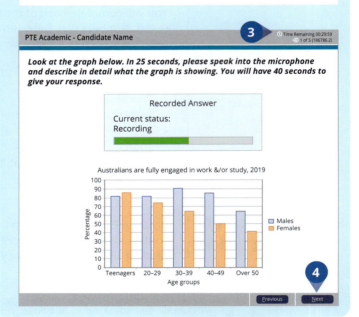

4. At the end of a task, click 'Next'.

Points to remember: Speaking tasks

- At the start of the test, the computer will help you to check your headphones and microphone are set up correctly.
- You should speak in a natural voice at a normal speed and volume.
- Speaking too loudly or too quietly can affect your speaking score. A very high volume can distort the recording and a very low volume may not be picked up by the microphone.
- During tasks, it is a good idea to regularly check the timer so you know how much time remains. However, do not stop speaking while checking the time.
- When recording, the microphone will stop recording if you are silent for more than three seconds.
- You can use the erasable booklet and pen to take notes.

Personal introduction

 Time to give your response: 30 seconds
Number of these tasks in each test: 1

Personal introduction is your opportunity to briefly introduce yourself.
- You have 25 seconds to read the instructions and ideas for things to talk about.
- You should then speak into the microphone, talking about yourself.
- **This task is not scored.** You can send it, along with your Score Report, to the institutions of your choice.

1. The recording status box counts down from twenty-five seconds to zero. The status silently changes to 'Recording' (there is no tone). Start speaking when the bar begins moving. When the bar reaches the end, or when you've stopped speaking for three seconds, the microphone switches off and the status changes to 'Completed'.
2. Click 'Next' to go to the next task when you've finished speaking.

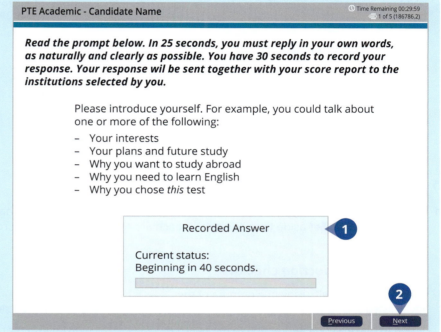

Strategies for success

This task allows you to warm up for the speaking sections and functions as an additional identity check for the test. You can also use it to introduce yourself to any institutions you are applying to. Use it to make a good impression and tell them about yourself.

Plan in advance what you want to talk about. Start by giving your name, and saying where you're from. Then, include some of the ideas from the instructions:

- **Your interests** • **Your plans for future study** • **Why you want to study abroad**
- **Why you need to learn English** • **Why you chose this test**

 Spend time before the test practising your introduction. Time yourself and make sure your message takes as close to 30 seconds as possible.

 You want to sound natural. Try not to write a speech and memorise it – this can often sound very unnatural and nerves on the day might make you forget the exact words you rehearsed. Instead, practise the kinds of things you want to say.

 Record yourself speaking, then listen to your introduction. If you were an admissions officer, would your message make a positive impression?

Practice 〉 Personal introduction

Here is a sample *Personal introduction* question for you to practise.

 Practise this task here, if you want to try *Personal introduction* without a time limit. Think about the strategies on page 23. Then follow the task instructions and record your response on your mobile phone or other device.

 Find this task in the **Online Question Bank** to complete it under timed conditions. Use the model answer that appears and compare it to your own response.

> **Read the prompt below. In 25 seconds, you must reply in your own words, as naturally and clearly as possible. You have 30 seconds to record your response. Your response will be sent together with your score report to the institutions selected by you.**
>
> Please introduce yourself. For example, you could talk about one of more of the following:
> - Your interests
> - Your plans and future study
> - Why you want to study abroad
> - Why you need to learn English
> - Why you chose *this* test

〉 Reflecting on your practice

1 Play back and listen to your response. Use the checklist below to decide what you did well and what you need to practise more. Set aside time to work on each area that you want to improve.

Personal introduction checklist

I spoke about myself, using one or more of the ideas listed	○	I spoke normally – not too loud, not too quiet, not too fast, not too slow.	○
I tried to make a good impression to my selected institutions.	○	I didn't pause for too long.	○
		I finished within 30 seconds.	○

2 🔊 Listen to a model answer for this task. Compare it to your own response. What are the differences? Are you happy with your response? What would you change?

 For more practice with *Personal introduction* and to hear sample answers, go to the **Online Question Bank**.

 Go to the **Online Resources** for extra study tools, including tips on *Improving Speaking Skills*.

24 | PERSONAL INTRODUCTION

Read aloud

 Preparation time: 30–40 seconds

Time to read the text aloud: 30–40 seconds

Number of these tasks in each test: 6–7

In *Read aloud* tasks, you read a short text out loud. How well you can do this shows how well you understand the text.

- You will see instructions, a recording status box and a short text.
- You have 30–40 seconds to prepare. Then read the text aloud into the microphone.
- This task tests your reading and speaking skills (pronunciation, intonation, rhythm, stress, linking and fluency).

1. The timer shows the time left for all tasks in this part of the test.
2. Read the task instructions.
3. The recording status box tells you how much time you have left to prepare.
4. After 30–40 seconds, the recording status box changes to 'Recording'. You have another 30–40 seconds to read the text aloud. The recording status box then changes to 'Completed' and the recording stops.
5. Click 'Next' to go to the next task.

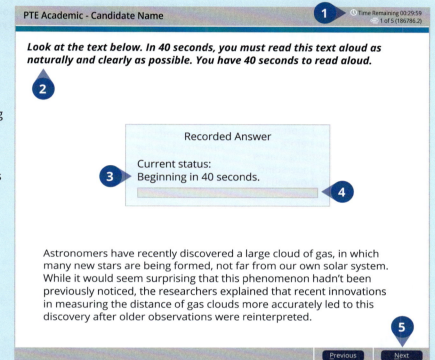

Skills tested

❯ Reading
- Understanding overall meaning
- Understanding specific information and details
- Identifying a writer's purpose, style, tone or attitude
- Understanding academic vocabulary
- Reading a text under timed conditions

❯ Speaking
- Speaking fluently at a natural speed
- Using clear pronunciation
- Using appropriate intonation (stress, rhythm and linking)
- Using a tone appropriate to the reason for speaking (e.g. to inform or to explain)

Points to remember: Speaking tasks

- You have a chance to **check your microphone** at the beginning. During all speaking tasks, keep your microphone the same distance from your mouth as it was during the microphone check. Also, speak at the same volume (not louder, not quieter).
- **Don't click 'Next' too soon.** Only move on to the next task when you are sure you are finished with the current one. You can't go back to these tasks to try again.

READ ALOUD | 25

Strategies for success › Before the test

You can improve your fluency, and get a better score, by learning about pauses, linking, intonation, and English rhythm.

4 Use intonation

The tone of your voice should usually fall at the end of each sense group.

If two things are contrasted, the first usually has rising intonation and the other usually has falling intonation.

In lists, each item usually has rising intonation except for the last, which has falling intonation.

3 Practise linking

This is the smooth joining together of words within a sense group. For example, in *have recently discovered*, all three words are pronounced together without pausing. To link vowel sounds together, use a *y* or *w* sound (e.g. *they*y*end*, *I*y*am* or *too*w*often*, *who*w*is*).

2 Speak with a good rhythm

In English, not every word or syllable is pronounced equally. Some words are pronounced weakly or disappear completely. We stress the words which carry the important information. This has an effect on rhythm patterns. There should be an equal amount of time between each stressed syllable. For example, if you say *She has an in*t*eresting house* or *She has a big house*, they should both take the same time. The word 'interesting' is pronounced so that it seems to only have three syllables and takes the same time to say as 'big'.

1 Split your sentences into sense groups

In the task on the previous page, the first part of the starting sentence is a sense group:

'*Astronomers have recently discovered a large cloud of gas*...' This is a sense group built around the verb 'discovered'. One word in this group is stressed more than the others ('gas') because this is the focus of the group.

We don't pause between the words in a group when speaking. However, we usually leave a very short pause after one sense group before starting a new one. Pausing makes it easier for people to understand you because you can show you have finished an idea.

› Practice tips

Record yourself on your mobile phone or other device as you practise reading aloud. Listen afterwards to your stress, intonation, rhythm and linking. If possible, compare the parts you found difficult to say with a fluent English speaker.

Pay attention to meaning while reading. If you understand the main idea of a text and which words carry the key information, you will sound more natural.

Learning academic vocabulary really helps with these tasks. Research shows that an excellent way to improve your vocabulary is to do lots of reading and listening on a range of different topics.

Find short texts from websites or in books. Mark a / (slash) after each sense group. Then read them, practising intonation, stress and rhythm as above.

Create lists of multi-syllable words. This can help you learn these patterns as well as the words themselves. For example, they could be in a table with words with a stressed first syllable in one column and words with a stressed second syllable in the next column, and so on.

› Language focus

Some words carry less weight than others when we read. Words like *to*, *of*, *on*, *they*, *have* are not usually stressed by a speaker and are shorter and quieter when you hear them. Nouns, verbs, adjectives and adverbs usually sound stronger and louder.

Also practise placing the stress on the correct part of words, e.g. *com*pen*sated*, *re*cent*ly*, *dis*cov*ered*, *infor*ma*tion*.

Your score for this task

COMMUNICATIVE SKILLS
Listening
Reading ✔
Speaking ✔
Writing

ENABLING SKILLS
Grammar
Oral Fluency ✔
Pronunciation ✔
Spelling
Vocabulary
Written discourse

Look out!

You will get a score of zero if you:
- say something that's different from the text on the screen (such as one you memorised before the test).

During the test

1 BEFORE READING ALOUD

Use the preparation time to look carefully at what you need to read and practise reading the text aloud.

- Most importantly, **think about meaning** – this will make it easier to read aloud naturally.
- **Look at where to group the words into sense groups**, to help you use stress, intonation and linking effectively.
- **Pay careful attention to how and where you will apply intonation, rhythm and pauses.** The commas and full stops will help a lot!
- **Think about which words to stress.** These are usually the nouns, verbs, adjectives and adverbs which carry important information.

2 WHILE READING ALOUD

Imagine you're **speaking to a friendly audience**.

Ignore other people in the room. Don't let their speaking distract you.

Speak normally – not too quiet, too loud, too fast or too slow. This should be the same volume as in the microphone check at the beginning of your test.

Pay attention to the meaning of what you're reading. If you focus carefully on what the text means, it's easier to use appropriate stress and intonation.

Try not to worry about words you don't know. Use your best guess at their pronunciation. If you focus too much on these words, you might sound unnatural.

Make sure you ...

✔ **only pause briefly.**
  ✘ Don't pause for longer than three seconds. The microphone switches off after three seconds of silence.

✔ **read exactly what you see on screen.**
  ✘ Don't skip any words. You won't get a mark if you miss a word or say a different one.

✔ **continue speaking, no matter what happens.**
  ✘ Don't correct yourself or start again if you make a mistake.

✔ **use natural pronunciation. This leads to a better performance.**
  ✘ Don't exaggerate your pronunciation or intonation. Speak as naturally as possible.

✔ **speak with a natural speed. It's fine to finish before the timer gets to zero.**
  ✘ Don't slow down just to fill the time.

✔ **pause when you see a comma, instead of saying 'comma'.**
  ✘ Don't say the name of the punctuation marks ('comma', full stop', etc.).

 Watch the *Read aloud: common mistakes* video for more tips and guidance on this task.

Practice > Read aloud

Here is a sample *Read aloud* question for you to practise.

 Practise *Read aloud 2* here, if you want to try *Read aloud* without a time limit. Think about the strategies on pages 26–27. Then follow the task instructions and record your response on your mobile phone or other device.

 Find *Read aloud 2* in the **Online Question Bank** to complete it under timed conditions.

> **Look at the text below. In 30 seconds, you must read this text aloud as naturally and clearly as possible. You have 30 seconds to read aloud.**
>
> Project management is an area of growing importance across many fields, from engineering and information technology through to education and marketing. Therefore, if you study this exciting subject, you will be opening the doors to a career with plenty of variety and excellent opportunities.

> Reflecting on your practice

1. Play back and listen to your response. Use the checklist below to decide what you did well and what you need to practise more. Set aside time to work on each area that you want to improve.

Read aloud checklist

I understood the text's overall meaning well during the preparation time.	○	I used appropriate rhythm and stress.	○
I understood the vocabulary in the text well during the preparation time.	○	I pronounced most words accurately.	○
I could mostly decide what stress, intonation, pauses, etc. to use.	○	I spoke normally – not too loud, not too quiet, not too fast, not too slow.	○
I paid attention to meaning while I was speaking.	○	I didn't pause too much, and I didn't miss out or repeat any words.	○
I used appropriate intonation on each sense group.	○	I gave my best guess for any words I didn't know how to pronounce.	○

2. 🔊 **Read aloud 2 model answer** Listen to a model answer for this task. Compare it to your own response. What are the differences? Are you happy with your response? What could you improve?

 For more practice with *Read aloud* tasks, go to the **Online Question Bank**.

 Go to the **Online Resources** for extra study tools. See the Speaking Resources for a *Read aloud Worksheet*, as well as *Useful Language for Speaking* and *Sample Answers & Feedback*.

Repeat sentence

Listening time: 3–9 seconds

Time to repeat the sentence: 15 seconds

Type of recording: audio only, single sentence

Number of these tasks in each test: 10–12

Repeat sentence tests your ability to reconstruct (through speaking) a sentence you hear using your knowledge of grammar and vocabulary.

- You will see instructions, an audio status box and a recording status box.
- You will hear a sentence.
- Repeat the sentence into the microphone exactly as you heard it.
- This task tests your listening and speaking skills (pronunciation, intonation, rhythm, stress, linking and fluency).

1. The timer shows the time left for all tasks in this part of the test.
2. Read the task instructions.
3. The audio status box counts down from three seconds to zero. Then you hear the sentence, followed by a one-second pause.
4. The recording status box changes to 'Recording'. Start speaking when the bar begins moving. When the bar reaches the end (after 15 seconds), or when you've stopped speaking for three seconds, the microphone switches off and the recording status box changes to 'Completed'.
5. Click 'Next' to go to the next task.

Skills tested

❯ Speaking

- Speaking fluently at a natural speed
- Using clear pronunciation
- Using appropriate stress, rhythm and linking
- Using appropriate intonation
- Using a tone appropriate to the reason for speaking (e.g. to inform or to explain)

❯ Listening

- Understanding overall meaning
- Understanding grammar
- Understanding academic vocabulary
- Understanding meaning from intonation, tone, etc.

Points to remember: Speaking tasks

- Some people speak quietly because they don't want to disturb other people during the test. Don't do this. If everything was OK during the microphone test, **speak normally and imagine the other people aren't there**.
- **Don't click 'Next' too soon.** Only move on to the next task when you are sure you are finished with the current one. You can't go back to these tasks to try again.

REPEAT SENTENCE | 29

Strategies for success ▸ Before the test

When getting ready for this task type, there are lots of things to keep in mind.

1 STAY FOCUSED

Be ready to listen carefully to the short sentence you are going to hear. It will be short (3–9 seconds) and you need to repeat every word you hear.

2 LISTEN CAREFULLY TO *HOW* THE SPEAKER SAYS THE SENTENCE.

Listen to the way the speaker phrases the words. Notice how the speaker uses intonation and syllable stress on long words such as *encouraged* and *activities*. Try to copy the same intonation and stress. However, you will not need to copy the speaker's accent. Just speak in your natural accent, but make sure your pronunciation is clear.

3 THINK ABOUT ANY WORDS YOU MISSED.

Many words in a sentence are unstressed. These are called 'weak forms' and may not be said clearly at all. For example, in the phrase *as a team*, the word 'team' is stressed, but the word 'a' might be very short and unclear. The words 'as a' may be linked together as if it's one word. Your knowledge of grammar should tell you that the word 'a' is present and that you need to include it when you repeat the sentence, with the same linking.

❯ Practice tips

Find some podcasts in English. Listen, pausing after each clause or short sentence. Repeat what you heard. Remember to do the following.

- **Train yourself to pay attention to meaning while listening.** If you understand the main idea behind the text, and which words carry the key information, you will sound more natural.
- **Try listening with and without note-taking.** Some people find that note-taking helps them, but others find it doesn't help. If you do take notes, only write the key words, as you won't have time to write the whole sentence.
- **Record yourself** on your mobile phone or other device as you practise repeating sentences. Listen afterwards to your stress, intonation and rhythm. Compare the parts you found difficult with the original recording.
- **Practise speaking with a good rhythm** in English. There should be equal time between stressed syllables, whether they are close together or far apart. For example, if you say *She has an <u>interesting house</u>* or *She has a <u>big house</u>*, they should both take the same time to say. The word 'interesting' is pronounced so that it seems to only have three syllables and takes the same time to say as 'big'.

Try to learn academic words and collocations. It really helps with these tasks! Research shows that an excellent way to improve your vocabulary is to do lots of reading and listening on a range of different topics.

❯ Language focus

Practise linking words together. This is the smooth joining together of words within a group. For example, in the phrase *has an interesting* all three words are pronounced together without pausing.

Practise correct syllable stress, e.g. g<u>o</u>vernment, p<u>e</u>nalise, e<u>mi</u>ssions.

Note how a speaker uses sentence stress to highlight important information. Try to do the same.

Your score for this task

COMMUNICATIVE SKILLS
Listening ✔
Reading
Speaking ✔
Writing

ENABLING SKILLS
Grammar
Oral Fluency ✔
Pronunciation ✔
Spelling
Vocabulary
Written discourse

Look out!

You will get a score of zero if you:
- say a sentence that's different from the one you hear (such as one you memorised before the test).

 **During the test**

❶ WHILE LISTENING

The audio status box will count down from three seconds and then the recording will play.

Think about meaning while listening – this will make it easier to repeat the sentence naturally.

Pay attention **to intonation**, **linking**, **stress and rhythm**.

Generally, there is not enough time to take notes in this task. If, in earlier practice, you found that taking notes in these tasks worked for you, then take notes while you listen.

Only write down the key words rather than the whole thing.

If you decide not to take notes, **closing your eyes while listening could help you focus** on the recording.

Forming a 'picture' in your mind of the meaning of the sentence may also help.

❷ WHILE SPEAKING

Wait until the bar that shows the microphone is open, then speak. There is **no tone to indicate when the microphone activates**, so just start speaking when the status changes to 'Recording'.

Imagine you're **speaking to a friendly audience**.

Speak normally – not too quiet, too loud, too fast or too slow. This should be the same volume you used when checking your microphone at the beginning of the test.

Pay attention to meaning. If you focus carefully on what the text means, it's easier to use appropriate stress and intonation. It might help if you remember the 'picture' that you formed in your mind while listening.

Try not to worry about words you don't know. Say them as closely as you can to how you heard them. If you focus too much on these words, you'll sound unnatural, which might reduce your score.

If you make a mistake, stay calm and continue speaking. Most people will make some mistakes. Try not to repeat anything, because you will lose marks if you do.

Make sure you …

✓ **only pause briefly.**
  ✗ Don't pause for longer than three seconds. The microphone switches off after three seconds of silence.

✓ **try to repeat all the words.**
  ✗ Don't skip any words. You won't get a mark if you miss a word or say a different one.

✓ **try to just continue speaking, no matter what happens.**
  ✗ Don't correct yourself or start again if you make a mistake.

✓ **use natural pronunciation. It leads to a better performance.**
  ✗ Don't exaggerate your pronunciation or intonation.

✓ **speak with a natural speed. It's fine to finish before the timer gets to zero.**
  ✗ Don't slow down just to fill the time.

✓ **copy the intonation and stress you heard.**
  ✗ Don't try to copy the accent you hear. Any clear accent is fine.

 Watch the *Repeat sentence: common mistakes* video for more tips and guidance on this task.

Practice 〉 Repeat sentence

Here is a sample *Repeat sentence* task for you to practise.

 Practise *Repeat sentence 2* here, if you want to try *Repeat sentence* without a time limit. Think about the strategies on pages 30–31. Then follow the task instructions and record your response on your mobile phone or other device.

 Find *Repeat sentence 2* in the **Online Question Bank** to complete it under timed conditions.

🔊 Repeat sentence 2 **You will hear a sentence. Please repeat the sentence exactly as you hear it. You will hear the sentence only once.**

〉 Reflecting on your practice

1 Play back and listen to your response. Use the checklist below to decide what you did well and what you need to practise more. Set aside time to work on each area that you want to improve.

Repeat sentence checklist

I understood the sentence's overall meaning well while listening.	○	I used appropriate intonation on each piece of information.	○
I understood the vocabulary in the sentence well while listening.	○	I spoke normally – not too loud, not too quiet, not too fast, not too slow.	○
If I took notes while listening, they were only the key words.	○	I didn't pause too much, and I didn't miss out or repeat any words.	○
I paid attention to meaning while I was speaking.	○	I didn't correct myself or try to copy the accent I heard.	○
I pronounced most words accurately.	○	I gave my best guess for any words I didn't know how to pronounce.	○
I used appropriate rhythm and stress.	○		

2 🔊 Repeat sentence 2 model answer Listen to a model answer for this task and check the answer in the Answer key. Compare it to your own response. What are the differences? Are you happy with your response? What could you improve?

 For more practice with *Repeat sentence* tasks, go to the **Online Question Bank**.

 Go to the **Online Resources** for extra study tools. See the Speaking Resources for a *Repeat sentence Worksheet*, as well as *Useful Language for Speaking* and *Sample Answers & Feedback*.

Describe image

 Preparation time: 25 seconds

Time to describe the image: 40 seconds

Number of these tasks in each test: 6–7

Describe image tests your ability to describe the information in an image of a graph, chart, map, table or picture.

- You will see the image.
- After 25 seconds, you should give a spoken description of the information in the image.
- Your speaking skills are tested.

1. The timer shows the time left for all tasks in this part of the test.
2. The recording status box counts down from 25 seconds to zero.
3. The recording status box changes to 'Recording'. Start speaking when the bar begins moving. When the bar reaches the end (after 40 seconds), or when you've stopped speaking for three seconds, the microphone switches off and the recording status box changes to 'Completed'.
4. Click 'Next' to go to the next task.

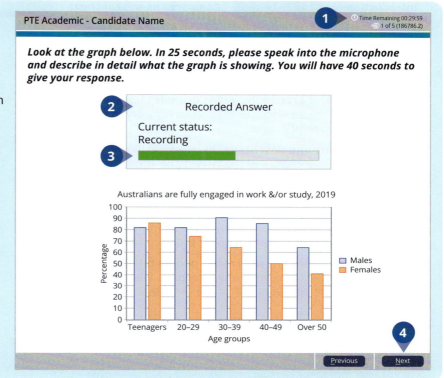

Skills tested

❯ Speaking

- Speaking under timed conditions
- Using supporting details (e.g. numbers) and explanations
- Organising a short oral presentation in a logical way
- Developing complex ideas within a short talk
- Using words and phrases appropriate to the context
- Using accurate grammar

- Speaking fluently at a natural speed
- Using clear pronunciation
- Using appropriate intonation, stress, rhythm and linking
- Using a tone appropriate to the reason for speaking (e.g. to inform or to explain)

Points to remember: Speaking tasks

- **Take time to get familiar with the mechanics of each speaking task** and what happens on screen, as well as what you need to do or say. Managing the task itself can affect how successfully you complete it. Pay attention to when the computer will start recording and when you need to start speaking, as well as how much time you have for your responses.

- **Don't click 'Next' too soon.** Only move on to the next task when you are sure you are finished with the current one. You can't go back to these tasks to try again.

DESCRIBE IMAGE | 33

Strategies for success » Before the test

Practise organising your descriptions into a logical structure.

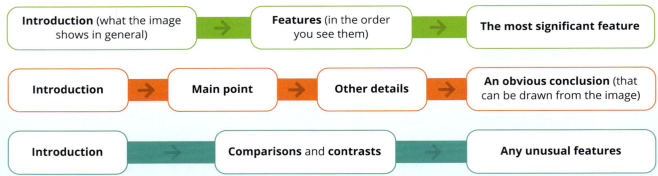

» Practice tips

Find some graphs, charts, maps, plans or tables from books, newspapers, academic or government websites to practise with. Try to find a variety of examples of each type of image.

Practise identifying and describing the most significant features of an image (e.g. the biggest change or the largest and smallest differences) and the relationships between them.

Record yourself on your mobile phone or other device as you practise describing graphs, charts, etc. Listen afterwards to the organisation of your talk, and to your stress, intonation, rhythm and pronunciation. Start with untimed practice and later practise under timed conditions.

Practise in an environment with other people talking around you – for example, with the TV / radio on or in a busy place with other people around. There are likely to be people talking at the same time as you in the PTE-A exam room.

Practise drawing conclusions. For example, if the image shows that more people take trains than buses in a particular city, the conclusions at the end of your talk might be:

> This suggests that the city's train network might be more convenient for commuters than the bus network.

The conclusions should be logical and reasonable given the data.

Practise giving implications. In the example above, you could say: *If you visit this city, you're more likely to travel by train than by bus.*

Practise intonation when describing images. Note that:
- the tone of voice usually falls at the end of each point.
- if two things are contrasted, the first point usually has rising intonation and the second usually has falling intonation. For example,

> While the number of women in employment rose, the corresponding number of men fell.

» Language focus

Study a range of words, collocations and grammatical structures for describing different features of the various types of images, e.g.

- statistical vocabulary to describe trends (synonyms for *increase*, *decrease*, etc.);
- comparative and superlative structures for pie charts, line graphs with two or more lines, (e.g. *far more than*);
- directions and locations for maps;
- estimates of quantity (e.g. *roughly, around, just below*);
- other useful phrases: *a significant percentage of, reached a peak of nearly 27.5 million in 2005, miles per hour, in comparison, 1997 saw a much smaller increase, a little to the north west of,* etc.

Your score for this task

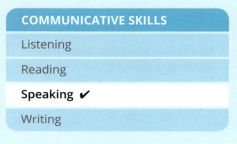

Look out!

You will get a score of zero if you:
- describe information that isn't relevant to the image
- give an answer you have memorised before the test

 **During the test**

1 BEFORE DESCRIBING THE IMAGE

Use the 25 seconds preparation time to analyse the image carefully.

- **Take notes**, using the erasable booklet and pen, if you have practised taking notes while doing these tasks and they help you speak. Only write **key words**, you won't have time to write full sentences.
- **Identify the general topic and type of information in the image**. Check the title, the axes (for graphs and charts), the headings and sub-headings (for tables) or the labels (for maps and pictures).
- **Check the units of measurement used** (US dollars, kilograms, etc.) and the reference points (years, categories, etc.).
- **Identify the important features and the relationships between them**. If it is a graph, a chart or a table, look for a trend you can comment on. If it is a map, flow chart or picture, comment on the important features.
- **Draw a conclusion** or work out an implication.
- **Think about how to describe it logically**. For example, don't plan to start on one side of the image and work your way to the other side – you may run out of time before you finish. It is more important to describe key parts than to describe everything you see.
- When the count down has nearly reached zero, **take a deep breath** so you're ready to start speaking.

2 WHILE DESCRIBING THE IMAGE

When you hear the tone, start speaking **straight away** (the microphone switches off if you don't say anything within three seconds).

Speak normally, clearly and naturally – not too quiet, too loud, too fast or too slow. This should be the same volume you used when checking your microphone at the beginning of the test.

Some people feel uncomfortable speaking just to the microphone, so **imagine you're speaking to a friendly audience**.

Ignore others in the room. Don't let their speaking distract you.

Pay careful attention to intonation, rhythm, pauses, etc.

3 FOLLOW A PLAN

Describe the content of the image, e.g. *The map shows ...*

Summarise the most significant features with supporting details. For example, *The highest temperature of 32 degrees was reached in the middle of summer, as seen in the graph in the month of July.*

Avoid repeating information.

Pay attention to time and give your conclusion or implication before your 40 seconds of speaking time is finished.

Make sure you ...

✓ **only pause briefly.**
  ✗ Don't pause for longer than three seconds. The microphone switches off after three seconds of silence.

✓ **focus on the most relevant information.**
  ✗ Don't try to give all the information you can think of. It will be too difficult and won't help you achieve your goal.

✓ **use natural pronunciation.**
  ✗ Don't exaggerate your pronunciation or intonation.

✓ **only use the information provided, even if you know other things about the topic.**
  ✗ Don't use your own knowledge on a topic to describe the image.

✓ **build your response using the details in the image and the useful language you know for describing.**
  ✗ Don't give a response you memorised before the test as you may go off topic. You will get a very low score (or zero) for this.

✓ **try to talk about different parts of the image and vary how you are describing or comparing the information.**
  ✗ Don't repeat information.

 Watch the *Describe image: Common mistakes* video for more tips and guidance on this task.

Practice 〉 Describe image

Here is a sample *Describe image* task for you to practise.

 Practise *Describe image 2* here, if you want to try *Describe image* without a time limit. Think about the strategies on pages 34–35. Then follow the task instructions and record your response on your mobile phone or other device.

 Find *Describe image 2* in the **Online Question Bank** to complete it under timed conditions.

Look at the graph below. In 25 seconds, please speak into the microphone and describe in detail what the graph is showing. You will have 40 seconds to give your response.

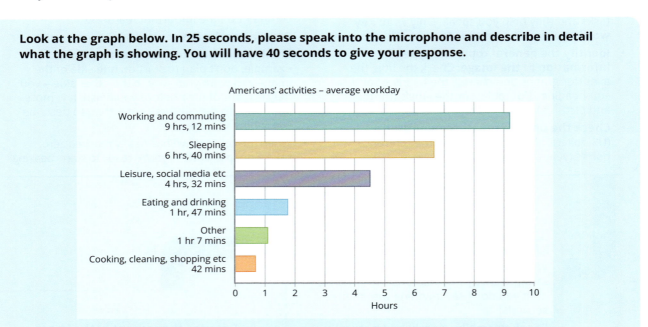

〉 Reflecting on your practice

1 Play back and listen to your response. Use the checklist below to decide what you did well and what you need to practise more. Set aside time to work on each area that you want to improve.

Describe image checklist

I identified the topic and the important features in the preparation time.	○	I used appropriate pronunciation.	○
I made a plan and followed it in my response.	○	I spoke normally – not too loud, too quiet, too fast or too slow.	○
I described the main features of the image.	○	I didn't pause too much and I didn't miss out or repeat any words.	○
I gave supporting details (e.g. numbers, facts).	○	I filled the time available and said everything I planned to say before the end.	○
I only included relevant information	○		
I gave a conclusion or an implication.	○		

2 🔊 `Describe image 2 model answer` Listen to a model answer for this task. Compare it to your own response. What are the differences? Are you happy with your response? What could you improve?

 For more practice with *Describe image* tasks, go to the **Online Question Bank**.

 Go to the **Online Resources** for extra study tools. See the Speaking Resources for a *Describe image Worksheet*, as well as *Useful Language for Speaking* and *Sample Answers & Feedback*.

36 | DESCRIBE IMAGE

Re-tell lecture

Length of video or audio: 50–90 seconds

Preparation time: 10 seconds

Time to re-tell the lecture: 40 seconds

Type of recording: audio or video, part of a lecture

Number of these tasks in each test: 3–4

Re-tell lecture tests your ability to summarise the important points from part of a lecture in your own words.

- You will see instructions, an audio status box and a recording status box.
- You will hear information from a short piece of audio or a video. If it is audio-only, there will be an image related to the topic of the lecture.
- You should re-tell the main points of the lecture using the microphone.
- This task tests your listening and speaking skills.

1. The timer shows the time left for all tasks in this part of the test.
2. Read the instructions.
3. The audio status box counts down from three seconds to zero.
4. Then the video or audio starts. Watch the video or look at the image to help you understand the topic of the recording. Start planning your response.
5. The recording status box changes to 'Recording'. Start speaking when the bar begins moving. When the bar reaches the end, or when you've stopped speaking for three seconds, the microphone switches off and the recording status box changes to 'Completed'.
6. Click 'Next' to go to the next task.

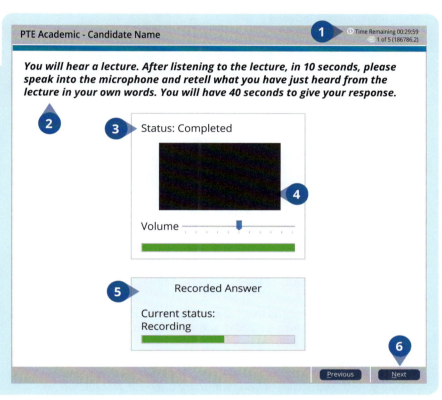

Skills tested

› Listening

- Identifying the main ideas and supporting points
- Identifying the speaker's purpose, style, tone or attitude
- Understanding academic vocabulary
- Inferring the meaning of unfamiliar words
- Comprehending explicit and implicit information

› Speaking

- Organising opinions or points with details, examples and explanations under timed conditions
- Using appropriate words, phrases and grammar
- Speaking fluently at a natural speed with clear pronunciation and intonation
- Using an appropriate tone for the context

Points to remember: Speaking tasks

- Some speaking tasks focus only on speaking while others assess integrated skills. So, depending on the task you may only need to speak, or listen and then speak, or even take notes while you are listening to help you speak afterwards. It is important to practise different ways of doing each task type to find an approach you are comfortable with.

RE-TELL LECTURE | 37

Strategies for success › Before the test

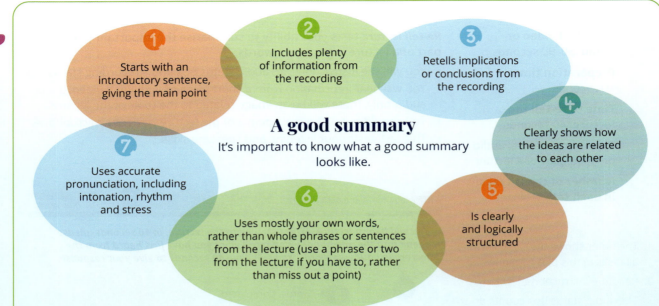

› Practice tips

Find some online videos (e.g. formal talks, discussions or university lectures) **or academic podcasts** on general topics. Choose ones that give information, but avoid news websites as these are different from what you will hear in the test. Listen to 50–90 seconds of a video and do the following:

- Identify the main points of the talk, any examples or evidence, and any opposing arguments.
- Listen for the signal words that indicate the main points (e.g. *We need to focus on …, The issue here is …, What we've discovered is …, For instance, To illustrate, On the contrary*, etc.).
- Make sure you understand these expressions, as they can help you identify key information when listening. They can also help you to make sure the structure of your summary is logical. Note down any new expressions and learn them.

You will need to take notes, to help you remember all the main points you hear. **Create your own techniques for quick note-taking.**

- Choose your own abbreviations and symbols and practise using them so that they become automatic.
- Practise writing the key words of main ideas and important details.

Practise in an environment with other people talking around you – for example, with the TV and/or radio on. There are likely to be people talking at the same time as you in the PTE-A test room.

› Language focus

Learn academic vocabulary as it will really help with these questions, both with understanding the lecture and using your own words to express the ideas you heard.

- Listen for any unfamiliar words and try to guess their meaning from the words around them. Check your guesses in a dictionary.
- Create lists of words with their synonyms. A thesaurus will help you to find new words with the same or similar meanings.
- When you learn a new word, record an example of how it's used in context.

Your score for this task

COMMUNICATIVE SKILLS
Listening ✔
Reading
Speaking ✔
Writing

ENABLING SKILLS
Grammar
Oral Fluency ✔
Pronunciation ✔
Spelling
Vocabulary
Written discourse

Look out!

You will get a score of zero if you:
- describe information that isn't relevant to the lecture (such as an answer you memorised before the test).

38 | RE-TELL LECTURE

> During the test

1 BEFORE LISTENING
Look at the image or the part of the video you can see. This will give you an idea of the general topic and help you to predict what you will hear. Be quick – you only have three seconds before the recording starts.

2 WHILE LISTENING
Take notes using the erasable booklet and pen, focusing only on key words.
Listen out for signalling words and expressions. These will help you identify the main points and relationships between ideas.

3 BEFORE RE-TELLING THE LECTURE
Quickly review your notes when the audio stops, and plan your talk. You have ten seconds to do this. Think about what you need to include:
- **an introductory sentence** to begin your talk, giving the main point;
- **important details**. Also think about what not to include (as you only have 40 seconds to re-tell the lecture);
- **relationships between ideas** (e.g. signalling that something you say is an implication or conclusion).

When the count down is nearly at zero, take a deep breath so that you're ready to start speaking.

4 WHILE RE-TELLING THE LECTURE
Follow your plan, using your notes.
- **Give the introductory sentence**, expressing the main point.
- **Include all the most important points** in the lecture and their relationships.
- **Make clear the relationships** between the ideas you heard. For example, if you heard a conclusion, say *in conclusion* before repeating it.
- **Pay careful attention to intonation, rhythm, pauses**, etc.

- Some people feel uncomfortable speaking into the microphone, so **imagine you're speaking to a friendly audience**.
- **Speak normally, clearly and naturally** – not too quiet, loud, fast or slow. Speak at the same volume as in the microphone check at the beginning of the test.
- **Pay attention to time** and make sure you explain all the main points and the relationships between them, including any conclusions or implications, before your 40 seconds speaking time is finished.

Make sure you ...

✔ **use your own note-taking technique that helps you focus on the important details.**
  ✘ Don't write down every word. You may miss important information if you focus more on writing than listening.

✔ **start speaking as soon as you hear the tone and only pause briefly.**
  ✘ Don't pause for longer than three seconds. The microphone switches off after three seconds of silence.

✔ **only use information from the audio. It will provide all the information you need.**
  ✘ Don't add any of your own knowledge, opinions, ideas or evaluation. Your score will be affected if you go off-topic.

✔ **continue speaking, even if you are finding it difficult or make a mistake.**
  ✘ Don't start again if you make a mistake.

✔ **build your response using the information you heard in the lecture.**
  ✘ Don't give a response about something else. Talking about different information, even if the topic is similar, might affect your score.

✔ **use your own words to summarise the lecture.**
  ✘ Don't use too many words from the lecture.

✔ **use natural pronunciation.**
  ✘ Don't exaggerate your pronunciation or intonation.

✔ **cover all the main points of the lecture in order.**
  ✘ Don't repeat information.

 Watch the *Re-tell lecture: common mistakes* video for more tips and guidance on this task.

Practice › Re-tell lecture

Here is a sample *Re-tell lecture* question for you to practise with.

Re-tell lecture 2 Practise *Re-tell lecture 2* here, if you want to try *Re-tell lecture* without a time limit. Think about the strategies on pages 38–39. Then follow the task instructions and record your response on your mobile phone or other device.

Find *Re-tell lecture 2* in the **Online Question Bank** to complete it under timed conditions.

🔊 **Re-tell lecture 2** **You will hear a lecture. After listening to the lecture, in 10 seconds, please speak into the microphone and retell what you have just heard from the lecture in your own words. You will have 40 seconds to give your response.**

› Reflecting on your practice

1 Play back and listen to your response. Use the checklist to decide what you did well and what you need to practice more. Set aside time to work on each area that you want to improve.

Re-tell lecture checklist

I could use the image or video still to predict the topic of the lecture.	○	I only included relevant information.	○
I listened carefully and identified key points.	○	I gave the main points and the relationships between them.	○
I took notes using the note-taking technique I'd practised before the test.	○	I used appropriate intonation, rhythm and stress.	○
		I pronounced most words accurately.	○
I planned my talk before I started speaking.	○	I spoke normally – not too loud, quiet, fast, or too slow.	○
I followed my plan in my talk.	○	I didn't pause too much and I didn't miss out or repeat any words.	○
I started with a sentence giving the main point of the lecture.	○		
I gave the important details.	○	I filled the time available and said everything I planned to say before the end.	○

2 🔊 **Re-tell lecture 2 model answer** Listen to a model answer for this task. Compare it to your own response. What are the differences? Are you happy with your response? What could you improve?

For more practice with *Re-tell lecture* tasks, go to the **Online Question Bank**.

Go to the **Online Resources** for extra study tools. See the Speaking Resources for a *Re-tell lecture Worksheet*, as well as *Useful Language for Speaking* and *Sample Answers & Feedback*.

Answer short question

Time to give your response: 10 seconds

Number of these tasks in each test: 10–12

Type of recording: audio only, single question

Answer short question tests your ability to answer a question using the right vocabulary.

- You will see instructions, an audio status box and a recording status box.
- You will hear a question.
- You should give a short answer (just one or a few words) using the microphone.
- This task tests your listening and speaking skills, as well as your vocabulary.

1. The timer shows the time left for all tasks in this part of the test.
2. Read the task instructions.
3. The audio status box counts down from three seconds to zero. Then you hear a question, followed by a one-second pause.
4. The recording status box changes to 'Recording'. Start speaking when the bar begins moving. Give your answer into the microphone (just one or a few words is fine). When the bar reaches the end (after 10 seconds), or when you've stopped speaking for three seconds, the microphone switches off and the recording status box changes to 'Completed'.
5. Click 'Next' to go to the next task.

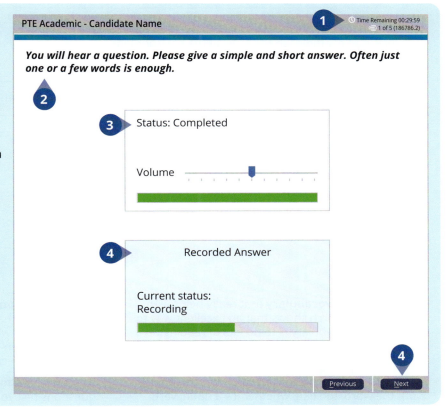

Skills tested

› Speaking

- Speaking for a purpose (e.g. to inform)
- Using appropriate words and phrases
- Speaking without preparation

› Listening

- Understanding detailed information
- Understanding academic vocabulary
- Inferring the meaning of unfamiliar words

Points to remember: Speaking tasks

- Some people speak quietly because they don't want to disturb other people during the test. Don't do this – **speak normally and imagine the other people aren't there**. If everything was OK during the microphone check, your natural speaking voice should be fine.

- **Don't click 'Next' too soon.** Only move on to the next task when you are sure you are finished with the current one. You can't go back to these tasks to try again.

Strategies for success › Before the test

A good way to expand your vocabulary is by using diagrams. Use these to build up your knowledge of word forms. A thesaurus and dictionary can help you to add more words.

Start with a common word, (e.g. *pollution*), and put this at the top of your diagram. You can then show the different parts of speech of this word, along with example sentences.

pollution

pollute (v) Chemicals from factories can pollute the air we breath.

polluted (adj) The river is now so polluted that fish cannot live in it.

You can also create diagrams to extend your vocabulary on a topic. Here is an example, on the topic of the environment.

- environment
  - pollution
    - air
    - water
    - noise
  - energy
    - renewable energy
    - solar power
    - fossil fuels

› Practice tips

Learn academic vocabulary as it really helps with these tasks! Research shows that an excellent way to improve your vocabulary is to do lots of reading on a range of different topics.

While reading, **note down new words** you find in a vocabulary notebook. Record other information about the word, too (e.g. whether it's a noun, verb or adjective, countable or uncountable, etc). Include example sentences in your notebook.

Focus on learning the right vocabulary. Don't spend too much time on technical words that you might never use. Focus on broadening your vocabulary in general across a lot of topics and learning words that might be used frequently in an academic context.

Record the pronunciation of new words. Use a dictionary that has a recording of the words and make sure you know where the stress is placed. This may change between noun, verb and adjective forms. For example: **ex**trovert, extro**ver**sion, extro**ver**ted.

Don't worry about your general knowledge. These questions test your English, not your knowledge. They can be answered just by using the general knowledge that most people have.

Find question lists. Practise answering your own questions or by using the questions on the Online Question Bank.

Your score for this task

COMMUNICATIVE SKILLS
Listening ✔
Reading
Speaking ✔
Writing

ENABLING SKILLS
Grammar
Oral Fluency
Pronunciation
Spelling
Vocabulary ✔
Written discourse

Look out!
You will get a score of zero if you:
- don't speak for 3 seconds (the microphone closes after 3 seconds of silence).
- don't speak clearly enough. The system won't recognise your answer.

42 | ANSWER SHORT QUESTION

 **During the test**

1 BEFORE LISTENING

You only have three seconds before you hear the question, Make sure you're prepared and ready to answer the question.

2 WHILE LISTENING

Listen carefully to the question and decide the type of information it is asking for. For example, should your answer be a noun, a verb or an adjective?

Pay careful attention to stressed words in the questions. The stressed words usually carry the main meaning.

3 WHILE ANSWERING

There is no tone to indicate when the microphone opens, so **just start speaking** as soon as the status changes to 'Recording'.

Ignore other people in the room. Don't let their speaking distract you.

Speak normally – not too quiet, too loud, too fast or too slow.

You only need to **answer with one word or a short phrase**.

Try not to think too much about your answer to these tasks. If you need thinking time, just say something. The microphone will stay open – but will close after three seconds of silence or after 10 seconds in total, so be quick!

Try not to answer with words from the question.

If you make a mistake, stay calm and correct yourself. In *Answer short question* tasks, wrong answers are ignored and you will not lose points for them, so you can keep trying until you give a correct answer or run out of time. This is different from some of the other speaking tasks.

If you can't think of the answer, guess. There is no penalty if you are wrong, and you might be right!

Similarly, **if you think of a better idea after your first answer, give it quickly**, before the microphone closes.

Make sure you ...

✓ **start speaking straight after the question is finished.**
  ✗ Don't wait too long before you answer. The microphone activates one second after the question finishes.

✓ **think about the question as you hear it and form your answer.**
  ✗ Don't take notes. There is no time to review them.

✓ **speak naturally.**
  ✗ Don't worry about your accent. As long as your answer is clear, any accent is accepted.

✓ **speak clearly.**
  ✗ Don't speak too quietly, loudly, quickly or slowly. Your pronunciation is not scored in these tasks, but your answer must be clear for the system to recognise your voice.

✓ **keep guessing if you are unsure.**
  ✗ Don't stay silent. Making a guess has some chance of being correct and there is no penalty for saying something incorrect.

✓ **keep concentrating on the questions.**
  ✗ Don't relax yet. You have 10–12 of these tasks in the test. You can pause briefly after the last one.

 Watch the *Answer short question: common mistakes* video for more tips and guidance on this task.

Practice ❯ Answer short question

Here is a sample *Answer short question* task for you to practise.

 Practise this task here, if you want to try *Answer short question* without a time limit. Think about the strategies on pages 42–43. Then follow the task instructions and record your response on your mobile phone or other device.

 Find *Answer short question 2* in the **Online Question Bank** to complete it under timed conditions.

🔊 Answer short question 2   **You will hear a short question. Please give a simple and short answer. Often just one or a few words is enough.**

❯ Reflecting on your practice

1 Use the checklist below to decide what you did well and what you need to practise more. Set aside time to work on each area that you want to improve.

Answer short question checklist

I listened for the type of information the question was asking for.	○	I spoke normally – not too loud, not too quiet, not too fast, not too slow.	○
I understood the question's overall meaning well.	○	I didn't pause for too long.	○
I understood the vocabulary in the question well.	○	I quickly tried again if I made a mistake.	○
I responded as soon as the question finished.	○	I made guesses if I didn't know the answer straight away.	○
I pronounced the answer clearly.	○		

2 🔊 Answer short question 2 model answer   Listen to a model answer for this task and compare it to you own. Was your answer correct? How was your answer similar or different to the model answer?

 For more practice with *Answer short question* tasks, go to the **Online Question Bank**.

 Go to the **Online Resources** for extra study tools. See the Speaking Resources for an *Answer short question Worksheet*, as well as *Useful Language for Speaking and Sample Answers & Feedback*.

Building confidence: Speaking

› Effective speaking skills

To achieve your test score goals, you may need to improve your general speaking skills in English, which includes working on some of your enabling skills (vocabulary, grammar, pronunciation and oral fluency).

WELL-ORGANISED SPEECH

Not only *what* you say, but *how* it is organised can have an effect on how well you achieve a speaking goal.

Always have your purpose in mind when speaking. Remind yourself of the key points and information you need to include to express your ideas. This will help you present yourself in a clear and direct way.

Use preparation time to plan what you will say first and what will follow. This can help you to avoid false starts, hesitation or long when you speak.

Make sure you present your ideas logically and in a way that makes sense. This is easier said than done under pressure, but structuring what you say with an introduction, main body and conclusion can help you to organise your ideas.

State your purpose clearly. When starting to talk, make sure your first sentence states your main message clearly. This will set the scene for everything else you say and help you to stay focused on your goal.

Direct the listener through your ideas. Using signposting language such as *Moving on to the next point … An example of this is …* or *In conclusion …*, will help you to highlight key ideas and the relationship between them, as well as guide the listener to follow you.

Summarise what you have said to emphasise your main message. To make your summary as effective as possible, ask yourself what the key information is that you need to communicate, and how you can express it in the clearest way possible. This can be helpful with *Re-tell lecture* tasks.

Link ideas appropriately. Using linking words and expressions can help you to link ideas and produce well-connected speech.

USE AND CONTROL OF LANGUAGE

Using a wide range of words and phrases demonstrates a good level of English. Using specific terminology will help you communicate your message more accurately.

Expand your range of vocabulary for talking about familiar and unfamiliar topics. This is vital to your speaking skills and should be an ongoing and active learning process. Set targets for learning new words, phrases or expressions and make sure you are clear about the meaning of any new words you learn. This can help you to prepare for tasks where you need to focus on specific language use or meaning (such as *Re-tell lecture*, *Answer short question* and *Describe image*).

Choose words and expressions carefully as you speak. Some words can seem similar, but are used in different ways (e.g. *increase* and *build up*). Study and practise using synonyms and antonyms that you might want to use for specific purposes.

Assess your grammar knowledge. Refreshing your grammar knowledge and adding a greater variety of structures to your English will naturally improve your speaking skills. Identify tenses or grammar points that you find challenging and dedicate time to study them.

Learn specific grammar structures that help you to perform certain tasks. For example, ensuring you can confidently use comparatives and superlatives will help you talk about charts and graphs in *Describe image,* while learning reported speech will help with *Retell lecture*.

Use a variety of expressions to make your speech interesting. Using collocations and phrases will demonstrate that you have an understanding of how English is used by proficient speakers.

FLUENCY AND COHESION

How you speak can as important as the language you use.

Improve your pronunciation. Recording yourself practising the task types and listening back to check yourself is a good way to improve. Compare your answers with model answers, which can be found in the **Online Resources**.

Improve your pronunciation of difficult words. Make a list of sounds that you find challenging in English and isolate the consonant or vowel sounds you have difficulty with. Spend time practising the sounds on their own. When you are comfortable doing that, practise the sounds within the words.

Use appropriate sentence stress and rhythm. These are both key to shaping meaning in English. Listen to how proficient speakers use stress and rhythm to emphasise certain aspects of their speech. Being aware of how both work, can help you to express meaning in all speaking tasks.

Use intonation to divide up what you say. Look at how intonation separates sentences into meaningful segments. Using rising and falling intonation correctly can help the listener follow you more easily.

Practise speaking extensively on a topic at short notice. If you make mistakes, just keep going. This will help you speak spontaneously.

Think in English to speak in English. Trying to translate from your own language while speaking, can slow you down or cause problems in your English. Practise speaking in English without relying on your first language.

Control your speaking speed and use pauses. Where appropriate, this can help the listener to follow you and allow you to gather your thoughts for your next point. You can do this by paying attention to punctuation while reading (e.g. in *Read aloud* tasks) or thinking about where you might naturally pause when describing something (e.g. in *Describe image* tasks).

Use synonyms to avoid hesitation. If you forget the English word for something, use a synonym to keep your description concise and avoid hesitation.

For more support with speaking skills, go to to *Useful Language for Speaking* and *Improving Speaking Skills* in the **Online Resources**

BUILDING CONFIDENCE: SPEAKING

❭ Effective speaking skills checklist

Think about your speaking skills in English. Use this checklist to identify your strengths and areas where you could improve.

WELL-ORGANISED SPEECH

	I feel confident	I could practise more	I need to improve my skills
I am able to organise my thoughts quickly before I start speaking.	○	○	○
I start speaking by stating my main purpose.	○	○	○
I can organise my speech well by focusing on key points, giving details and examples to support what I say.	○	○	○
I can structure my arguments, ideas and descriptions logically in English.	○	○	○
I can structure sentences correctly in order to express meaning in a logical way.	○	○	○
I can begin to express my main idea or message clearly and precisely as soon as I start speaking.	○	○	○
I can use language efficiently to describe implications and summarise conclusions in a logical way.	○	○	○
I am able to identify key language on any topic that will help me describe it or talk about it.	○	○	○
I am familiar with specific phrases and useful language to guide the listener through what I am saying.	○	○	○
I can summarise an idea, retaining all of the key meaning and messages.	○	○	○
I can link my ideas together effectively.	○	○	○

USE AND CONTROL OF LANGUAGE

	I feel confident	I could practise more	I need to improve my skills
My vocabulary knowledge is varied enough for me to express ideas on any topic, with sufficient detail and precision.	○	○	○
I can understand unfamiliar vocabulary from its context.	○	○	○
I can use words and phrases appropriate to the context at hand.	○	○	○
I understand the subtle differences between some key words or phrases in English and how to apply them.	○	○	○
I am familiar with a range of synonyms and similar phrases that I can use to express ideas in a variety of ways.	○	○	○
I can develop a complex idea within a short space of time.	○	○	○
I can demonstrate good control of English by applying useful expressions and phrases that help convey my message.	○	○	○
I have good grammar and can use a variety of grammatical structures correctly to express my ideas well.	○	○	○
I have specific grammatical tools that help me to describe, contrast and compare information.	○	○	○
I can identify a formal or informal tone for speaking in different situations or with different purposes (e.g. to inform, explain or repeat information).	○	○	○

FLUENCY AND COHESION

	I feel confident	I could practise more	I need to improve my skills
I can speak clearly and articulate challenging words in English.	○	○	○
I can apply stress and rhythm effectively to convey meaning to the listener.	○	○	○
I can use specific language functions to link my ideas together, so they understandable to the listener.	○	○	○
I can pronounce most words accurately.	○	○	○
I have practised working with synonyms enough to be able to always find the words and phrases I need to express my ideas.	○	○	○
I try not to translate or think in my own language when speaking in English and thinking about how to express myself.	○	○	○
I am aware of the speed of my voice when speaking, and can control it and adapt it to what I am saying.	○	○	○
I can apply pauses in the right places to emphasise what I am saying.	○	○	○
I can speak confidently, even when I am unfamiliar with the topic or have little preparation time.	○	○	○

46 | EFFECTIVE SPEAKING CHECKLIST

❯ Building blocks for test confidence

1 **LISTENING SKILLS FOR SPEAKING**

Improving your general listening skills can help you prepare for speaking tasks, as many of the task types in PTE Academic require you to respond to something you hear (e.g. *Repeat sentence*). Improving your listening skills can help you to:
- identify the topic, theme or main ideas of what you are listening to;
- have a good chance of understanding what you hear in order to construct an appropriate response;
- understand vocabulary and its meaning from context, even when it is unfamiliar to you;
- identify information that is mentioned but not explicitly explained;
- learn to balance thinking about what to say with listening at the same time;
- identify key points necessary for constructing an appropriate response (e.g. *Re-tell lecture tasks*);
- pick up useful words, phrases and expressions to use when speaking;
- understand meaning from the intonation and tone of a speaker;
- follow oral sequencing of information and apply this to your own speech.

2 **NOTETAKING**

Notetaking can help you structure your speaking clearly and give you a point of reference so that you don't lose track of the ideas you want to express while speaking. In PTE Academic, notetaking is a good idea for some of the speaking tasks. It can be a useful strategy for gathering ideas together when under a strict time limit. In *Re-tell lecture*, for example, notetaking can help you catch all the key points from the audio track and then present them in your own words, all within the short space of time the task allows.

Try out different notetaking styles (such as spider charts, lists, visual representations of key points or bullet-pointed notes) and identify the notetaking method that works best for you. You may even want to develop your own techniques for rapid notetaking. Decide on your own abbreviations and symbols for getting points down quickly and practise using them.

3 **TIME MANAGEMENT**

For each speaking task, you only have a short time to prepare before recording your response. And some tasks often have strict time limits for recording your answer, which can make it difficult to fit everything you want to say into the available time.

Decide how you will use your preparation time for each task. Get used to this by practising giving responses within the time limits for each individual task (e.g. 10 seconds for preparation and 40 seconds for response in *Re-tell lecture* tasks; 25 seconds for analysis and 40 seconds for description in *Describe image* tasks).

4 **CRITICAL THINKING SKILLS**

You will need to think critically for some of the speaking tasks. Practise:
- analysing, comparing and interpreting text and graphic data;
- reflecting on a topic or information;
- applying reason to what you see or hear;
- structuring your arguments and thoughts on the information given.

❯ Keys for confidence

Embrace your mistakes, as this is the only way you can improve. Nobody can speak with effortless fluency at first.

Embrace your own way of speaking. Worrying about sounding like a native speaker will only mean you are more cautious. As long as you can be understood, speak in a way that is natural for you. This will allow you to express yourself more effectively

Practice makes for a good speaker. Surround yourself with English. Look for as many speaking opportunities as possible in order to work on improving your level.

Set yourself achievable speaking targets. Make a plan for improving the areas you have identified for working on your speaking skills and stick to it. You can't improve if you only practise your strengths. Set aside time each week to focus on your weak areas.

Don't be discouraged if speaking doesn't go as planned. Be confident, correct yourself if necessary while speaking and move on.

Part 1 | Writing

PART 1: WRITING

Overview

Sections 3–6 of Part 1, focus on writing tasks. These Sections test your ability to produce written academic English.

The total duration of the writing Section is **50–60 minutes**. There are **two task types in Sections 3-6:** *Summarize written text* and *Write essay*.

There are **two or three *Summarize written text*** tasks and **one or two *Write essay*** tasks (depending on which task the computer selects for Section 5). *Summarize written text* tasks are ten minutes each, while *Write essay* tasks are 20 minutes each.

Writing (Total time: 50–60 minutes)						
Sections 3–4	**Summarize written text**	2	After reading a passage, write a one-sentence summary.	Reading and writing	Text up to 300 words, answer up to 75 words	10 minutes each
Section 5	**Summarize written text or Write essay**	1	See above and below	Writing or Reading and writing	Word count depends on the task type	Timing depends on the task type
Section 6	**Write essay**	1	Write an essay of 200–300 words in response to a prompt.	Writing	Answer up to 300 words	20 minutes each

What is assessed in the Writing Sections

PTE Academic assesses a range of writing skills in this part of the test.

- Writing for a purpose (to inform, to persuade, to summarise)
- Supporting an opinion with details, examples and explanations
- Organising sentences and paragraphs in a logical way
- Developing complex ideas with a complete essay
- Communicating the main points of a written passage in writing
- Conveying degrees of certainty about ideas and opinions
- Synthesising information
- Writing to strict length requirements
- Using a range of vocabulary appropriate to the context
- Using correct grammar, spelling and punctuation
- Writing under timed conditions

Writing skills

Writing effectively begins with having a clear understanding of context. In PTE Academic, the context is academic writing, which is the style of writing expected within higher education. This differs from other styles of writing, such as fiction, emails and casual messages. Academic writing has a number of characteristics, including complexity, formality and objectivity. You should try to use a range of language to give your writing complexity. Formality can be achieved by avoiding colloquial language, such as the expressions used casually between friends. Formal language also does not usually include contractions (e.g. *can't, it'll*). As academic writing is usually objective rather than subjective, there are fewer words that refer directly to the writer or reader (e.g. words such as *I, my, you, your*).

48 | PART 1: WRITING

As well as context, successful writers have a clear understanding of their purpose when writing. The two writing tasks require you to write for different purposes. *Summarize written text* asks you to rephrase the main ideas of a passage into a short summary. In *Write essay* tasks, the requirement is to address a specific question in a well-developed and organised way, using supporting information. For both tasks, part of your purpose is to successfully use elements of written English, such as grammar and punctuation.

Developing writing skills starts with using simple phrases and sentences to describe familiar subjects. As we improve, we can link sentences together into paragraphs and then link paragraphs into longer pieces of writing, using appropriate connecting and reference words. The most advanced writers can produce clear, well organised and complex texts about a wide range of subjects. The goal is to use language concisely and precisely to convey different shades of meaning, and illustrate the relationships between different pieces of information.

What to expect in the writing section

These sections of the test assess how well you can write about academic topics. *Summarize written text* tasks feature authentic academic texts about a variety of topics from a range of academic disciplines, while *Write essay* tasks ask questions that could provoke academic debate. However, you do not need any prior knowledge of the topics presented. All of the information necessary to complete the tasks is presented within the passages. The topics have been selected in order to be equally familiar to the vast majority of test takers. *Write essay* tasks can be answered with basic general knowledge.

Using the authentic academic texts in PTE Academic helps test takers who will go on to study in higher education to prepare for exactly the kind of reading and writing they will do. The tasks directly match the demands of activities and assignments that you can expect to encounter during future studies. The skills you develop will also help you if you need to use English in a professional context.

Writing task types

Summarize written text involves reading a text on screen and then writing a short summary of it in your own words. It tests your ability to comprehend, analyse and combine information from a reading passage and then summarise the key points in writing. *Summarize written text* tasks require a short answer: a one-sentence summary of up to 75 words.

Write essay task involves reading a question on screen and then writing a response in essay format that addresses the question. The essay is scored based on a number of criteria, including structure and coherence, development of ideas, form, grammar, vocabulary and spelling. For *Write essay* tasks, you must write between 200 and 300 words.

During both writing tasks, you can use the erasable booklet and pen to make notes.

Scoring of writing tasks

Both writing task types contribute to your writing score, as well as scores for grammar and vocabulary. *Summarize written text* tasks contribute to reading scores, and *Write essay* tasks contribute to spelling and written discourse scores.

Task type	Overall score	Writing score	Reading score	Grammar score	Spelling score	Vocabulary score	Written discourse score
Summarize written text	✔	✔	✔	✔		✔	
Write essay	✔	✔		✔	✔	✔	✔

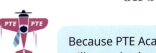

Managing the information on screen

During Sections 3-6 of PTE Academic, you will need to manage the time allocated for each task, type your responses into the space on screen and check your work carefully before submitting it.

Because PTE Academic is a computer-based test, you will use a keyboard to type your answers into the computer. You will use a QWERTY keyboard.

This is a keyboard design for Latin-script alphabets, where the order of the first six keys on first row of letters (from left to right) are: Q W E R T Y.

If you are not familiar with this type of keyboard, it is advisable to practice using one before taking the test if possible. Being comfortable typing in English will help you to perform to your best ability during the test.

1. During the writing tasks, you will be able to use your mouse to click and highlight text. There are 'Copy', 'Cut' and 'Paste' functions available during both tasks. This is a useful function that allows you to quickly move your own written text around, so you can rearrange or edit it quickly during the task.

2. You should monitor the 'Word Limit' counter to ensure you are within the required word count for each task. Remember that for *Summarize written text* tasks, be aware that you write a one-sentence summary of up to 75 words and for *Write essay* tasks, be aware that you must write between 200 and 300 words.

3. You can also monitor the timer throughout each task to check how much time remains.

Points to remember: Writing tasks

- Make sure you are addressing the question, not just writing about the topic.
- Write quickly and carefully to demonstrate the best of your writing skills within the time limit.
- Write within the word limit, or you will lose marks.
- Save a little time at the end of each task to proofread your work and check your grammar, spelling and punctuation. When proofreading, as well as looking for errors to correct, also look for opportunities to improve what you have written. For example, you might be able to add more formal or precise vocabulary.

Summarize written text

Length of text: up to 300 words

Reading and writing time: 10 minutes

Maximum number of words for response: 75

Number of these tasks in each test: 2–3

Summarize written text tests your ability to understand an academic text and give a summary of the most important points in one sentence.

- You will see instructions, a written text and a box to type your summary sentence into.
- You will have 10 minutes to read the text and to summarise it in **one sentence**.
- This task tests your reading, writing, grammar and vocabulary skills.

1. The timer counts down from 10 minutes which is the total time allowed for each *Summarize written text* task..
2. Read through the task instructions and the text.
3. Type your summary sentence into the box.
4. You can select text you have written in the box and use the 'Cut', 'Copy' and 'Paste' buttons to edit it.
5. The 'Total Word Count' shows the number of words in your sentence, and updates as you type.
6. Click 'Next' to go to the next task after you've checked your writing (otherwise, the test will automatically move forward to the next question after 10 minutes).

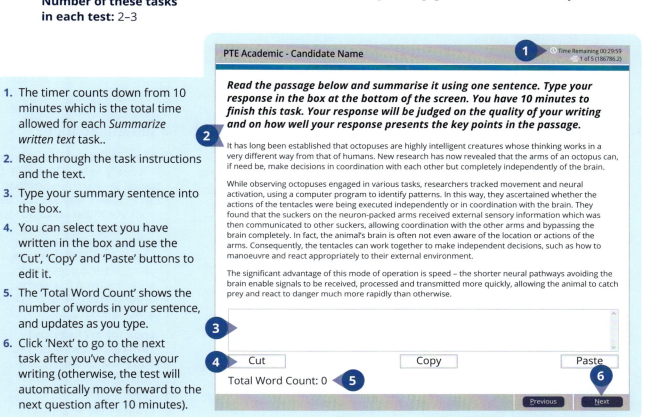

Skills tested

› Reading

- Reading under timed conditions
- Identifying main ideas, supporting points and specific details
- Identifying a writer's purpose or attitude
- Inferring the meaning of unfamiliar words
- Understanding explicit and implicit information
- Reading for overall organisation

› Writing

- Writing under timed conditions
- Writing a summary with a word limit
- Communicating the main points in writing
- Using appropriate vocabulary and grammar

Points to remember: Writing tasks

- Writing tasks **have specific requirements you must meet** in order to succeed in the task. Read the question carefully and make sure you understand its demands.
- You have 10 minutes for *Summarize written text* and 20 minutes for *Write essay* **to plan, write and check your work.** Use the time wisely.

SUMMARIZE WRITTEN TEXT | 51

Strategies for success > Before the test

Summary structure
A good written summary should:

1. include all the main points and any important supporting information but none of the minor points;
2. be presented in a logical order;
3. only include ideas from the text, not your own ideas;
4. be shorter than the original;
5. mostly use different words from the original.

› Practice tips

Practise summarising short texts from serious books or newspaper articles. Find some texts (2–5 paragraphs), giving information on a range of topics (e.g. science, technology, education, the environment). Then do the following.

- Find out the writers' main point and purpose (e.g. to inform, argue, warn, criticise, describe, persuade, explain, etc.)
- Practise locating topic sentences, which can help you to identify the main message.
- Identify cohesive devices. For example, highlight a word like *this* or *it* and then the idea it refers to. Or find a word for an idea that's repeated and then highlight each synonym of that word to follow the idea through the text.
- Review the uses of punctuation, especially the semi-colon (;). This is particularly useful for joining two related sentences to make one.

Become comfortable using a range of techniques in your writing. These will allow you to include more ideas into one sentence . Here are some examples.

- Use conjunctions (e.g. *also, because, for example, as a result of*, etc.).
- Use subordinate clauses (parts of a sentence that depend on another and can't exist alone). In the example below, the underlined subordinate clause doesn't make sense without the information at the beginning of the sentence.
  The reason people like PTE-A <u>is because it has several different types of tasks</u>.
- Use nominalisation (using nouns instead of verbs or adjectives, which can often sound more academic).
  <u>The intelligence</u> of octopuses is high.
  <u>Observations</u> of octopuses led to some interesting research.

› Language focus

Learn academic vocabulary – it really helps with these tasks! Research shows that an excellent way to improve your vocabulary is to do lots of reading on a range of different topics. Highlight any unfamiliar words in the texts you read and guess their meaning from the words around them. Then check in a dictionary.

Look for prefixes and suffixes. Knowing how to add these to base words will help to broaden your vocabulary.

Create lists of words with their synonyms. A thesaurus can help you to find new words with the same or similar meanings.

When you learn a new word, **record an example of how it's used in context**.

Your score for this task

COMMUNICATIVE SKILLS	ENABLING SKILLS
Listening	Grammar ✔
Reading ✔	Oral Fluency
Speaking	Pronunciation
Writing ✔	Spelling
	Vocabulary ✔
	Written discourse

Look out!
You will get a score of zero if you:
- write more than one sentence.
- don't write anything.
- use all capital letters.
- describe information that isn't relevant to the text, such as an answer you memorised before the test.

52 | SUMMARIZE WRITTEN TEXT

 **During the test**

1 BEFORE WRITING

First, **spend one minute skimming the text to understand the general topic**, then read carefully for the main ideas and key supporting ideas.

Take two minutes to read the passage more carefully and **make notes on the main and supporting ideas**, either mentally or in the erasable booklet.

Decide which information to include in your summary sentence, and which to miss out. You can't include everything, so choose wisely.

2 WHILE WRITING YOUR RESPONSE

Spend **five minutes writing** the one-sentence summary, and **two minutes comparing** your summary to the original passage.

Start with the main idea and then add supporting details. Imagine you are writing this summary for someone who has not seen the text.

Use a range of vocabulary. Remember to pack lots of information into the sentence. Try to paraphrase the text, rather than using the same words from the text.

If necessary, use a semi-colon (;) to **join two related sentences** into one.

Aim for a sentence that clearly conveys the main ideas. Don't make it too complicated. The maximum of 75 words is not a target. The best answers are usually much shorter than this. You don't get more points for using more words.

Make sure you really have **just one sentence**.

Use linking words to join two parts of a sentence together (e.g. *Octopuses are intelligent and they can do many things*.)

Move parts of the text around as much as you want using the 'Cut', 'Copy' and 'Paste' buttons.

Check the time as you write, to make sure you have time to complete the task and review it.

3 AFTER WRITING YOUR RESPONSE

Make changes where necessary.
Check the **content** of your summary.
- Does it communicate the main ideas?
- Does it only include the most important details?
- Does it flow smoothly and logically?

Check the **form** of your summary.
- Is it one single complete sentence?
- Is it 5–75 words?

Check **grammar, spelling and punctuation**.
- Does the sentence begin with a capital letter and end with a full stop?
- Have you written it in small letters, using capitals only where appropriate?

Make sure you …

✓ **stick to the key points.**
  ✗ **Don't** try to fit everything in the reading passage into the one-sentence summary.

✓ **clearly summarise the main points.**
  ✗ **Don't** try to make your summary long or too complicated. Remember that a good summary doesn't have to contain a lot of words.

✓ **check the number of words you are writing.**
  ✗ **Don't** use fewer than 5 or more than 75 words.

✓ **only summarise the information presented.**
  ✗ **Don't** add any of your own knowledge, opinion, ideas or evaluation.

✓ **answer the task question directly.**
  ✗ **Don't** give a response you memorised before the test. You will be summarising the wrong information even if the topic is similar.

✓ **use synonyms and paraphrasing, where possible.**
  ✗ **Don't** use exactly the same words as in the text.

 Watch the *Summarize written text: common mistakes* video for more tips and guidance on this task.

Practice › Summarize written text

Here is a sample *Summarize written text* question for you to practise.

 Practise *Summarize written text 2* here, if you want to try *Summarize written text* without a time limit. Think about the strategies on pages 52–53. Then follow the task instructions.

 Find *Summarize written text 2* in the **Online Question Bank** to complete it under timed conditions.

> **Read the passage below and summarise it using one sentence. You have 10 minutes to finish this task. Your response will be judged on the quality of your writing and on how well your response presents the key points in the passage.**
>
> A common experience for international students is the adjustment period when they move to a new environment and have to adapt to completely different educational, cultural or social settings, or a new language. Students can expect to feel anything from excitement and wonder to frustration and confusion, from anywhere between several weeks to several months. The common term for this is 'culture shock', and it typically stems from the challenges of learning what is appropriate in your new surroundings and what is not. The positive news is that this learning helps most people to develop a more flexible and open attitude, and with this you will be better able to meet these challenges and benefit from them.
>
> Typically, there are three distinct phases: the honeymoon, distress and recovery. In the initial phase, you enjoy the novelty of everything, feeling excited and confident. Before long, the second phase sets in and you begin to miss your usual way of life and question or even criticise the new environment. Being immersed in a different language starts to exhaust you, and your health may suffer. Fortunately, when you make it to the final phase the result is usually regained confidence and comfortable adjustment. You may even surprise yourself and find a new preference for some aspects of your new home.
>
> In order to reduce the experience of culture shock, there are some simple practices you can follow. Firstly, remember it is very common and there will be others who are going through something similar. You'll also benefit from sharing your experiences with friends and family. Make sure you keep to a healthy diet and exercise routine and get plenty of rest and recreation. Lastly, join some social clubs and make sure to explore your new home and learn as much as you can about it.

› Reflecting on your practice

1. Read your response. Use the checklist below to decide what you did well and what you need to practise more. Set aside time to work on each area that you want to improve.

Summarise written text checklist

I skimmed the text for the general topic, then read for main ideas, and supporting details.	○	I didn't misrepresent the topic or the purpose of the passage.	○
I understood the text's overall meaning well.	○	I checked my grammar, punctuation and spelling.	○
I understood the vocabulary in the text well.	○	I checked the word count.	○
I used accurate grammar, punctuation and spelling in my summary sentence.	○	I checked that the main idea and essential supporting points were included.	○
I used appropriate synonyms and paraphrasing.	○	I checked that my summary sentence flowed smoothly.	○

2. Read a model answer for this task in the Answer Key. Compare it to your own response. What are the differences? Are you happy with your response? What could you improve?

 For more practice with *Summarize written text* tasks, go to the **Online Question Bank**.

 Go to the **Online Resources** for extra study tools. See the Writing Resources for a *Summarize written text Worksheet*, as well as *Useful Language for Writing* and *How to Structure Academic Writing for Summaries*.

Write essay

Writing time: 20 minutes
Length of your essay: 200–300 words
Number of these tasks in each test: 1–2

Write essay tests your ability to write a short, persuasive or argumentative essay under strict time conditions.
- You will see an essay question.
- You will have 20 minutes to plan, write and revise an essay to address the question.
- Your writing skills are tested, along with your knowledge of grammar, vocabulary, spelling and written discourse.

1. The timer counts down from 20 minutes which is the total time allowed for each *Write essay* task.
2. Read the task instructions and the question.
3. Type your essay into the box.
4. You can select text you have written in the box and use the 'Cut', 'Copy' and 'Paste' buttons to edit it.
5. The 'Total Word Count' shows the number of words in your essay, and updates as you type.
6. Click 'Next' to go to the next task after you've checked your writing (otherwise, the test will automatically move to the next task after 20 minutes).

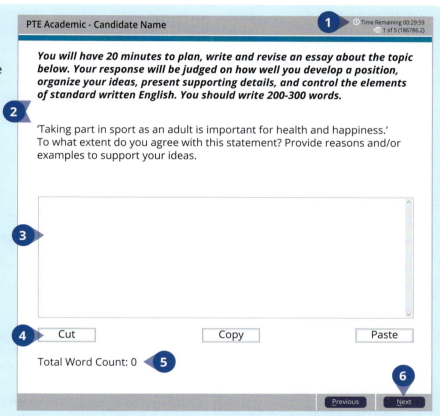

Skills tested

❯ Writing

- Writing for a purpose (e.g. to inform, to persuade)
- Supporting an opinion with details, examples and explanations
- Organising sentences and paragraphs in a logical way
- Developing complex ideas within a complete essay
- Using words and phrases appropriate to the context
- Using accurate grammar, spelling and punctuation
- Writing under timed conditions

Points to remember: Writing tasks

- It **doesn't matter if you are unfamiliar with the essay topic**. The essay questions are designed to be answered by most people with basic general knowledge. You don't need any special knowledge.
- **How you write and express ideas is being assessed**, not the opinion expressed in the writing. There are no right or wrong answers to this task and the opinion you express will not change your mark.

Strategies for success › Before the test

Approach essay writing by following the three steps.

1

Circle the topic in the essay question, then underline the part of the topic you must write about. For example, in the task on page 55, you could circle *taking part in sport as an adult* and underline *important for health and happiness*.

2

Identify the instruction that tells you exactly what to do (e.g. agree or disagree with a statement; argue for or against an opinion; discuss advantages and disadvantages, problems or solutions). In the task on page 55, the instruction is *To what extent do you agree with this statement? Provide reasons and/or examples to support your ideas*.

3

Create a plan for the topic and task.
Planning is very important in essay tasks. Make sure your text follows a logical structure.

1 Write a short introduction paragraph and:
  • start with one sentence that makes a general statement on the topic.
  • add a second sentence that introduces your opinion, argument or direction of the essay, focusing on the topic and the question.
2 Write two to three main paragraphs, focusing on your arguements and supporting statements
3 Finish with a short conclusion that summarises or re-states your main argument in one or two sentences.

› Practice tips

Spend some time brainstorming ideas for essay topics. You usually have to give **reasons for and against** an idea in essays, so practise thinking of arguments (reasons in favour of an opinion), counter-arguments (reasons against that opinion) and rebuttals (reasons why even the counter-arguments could be wrong).

Try writing main paragraphs first, then the introduction and conclusion last. Many people find this helpful. Practise different approaches and see which ones work for you.

Practise checking and editing your writing, especially for grammar, vocabulary and punctuation mistakes. Checking your own work is better than relying on a checking tool. Get used to identifying your weak areas and common mistakes as there won't be a spell-check function in the test.

Time yourself writing and completing essay tasks in 20 minutes with a maximum of 300 words. Work out how much time you should allocate to planning, writing and checking your essay and practise timing yourself with each part. It is also important to practise typing an essay quickly.

› Language focus

• Highlight any **unfamiliar words** in texts you read and guess their meaning from the words around them. Then check in a dictionary.
• **Create lists of words with their synonyms**. A thesaurus will help you to find new words with the same or similar meanings.
• When you learn a new word, **record an example of how it's used in context**. Also, record and learn which **suffixes and prefixes** are often added to the word.
• **Learn to use academic vocabulary**. Using a variety of language helps you express your ideas and avoid repeating words.
• **Learn signalling words and expressions** to help organise and link your arguments, such as *Firstly, Next, However, Moreover, On the other hand, Furthermore, In conclusion,* etc.

 ## Your score for this task

COMMUNICATIVE SKILLS
Listening
Reading
Speaking
Writing ✔

ENABLING SKILLS
Grammar ✔
Oral Fluency
Pronunciation
Spelling ✔
Vocabulary ✔
Written discourse ✔

Look out!

You will get a score of zero if you:
• write a very short or long essay.
• don't use punctuation.
• only write bullet points or very short sentences.
• only use capital letters.
• write a response which is not focused on the question.

> **During the test**

1 BEFORE WRITING

Read the essay question carefully. Identify the general topic and then identify exactly what the essay asks you to do.

Use the timer. Decide how much time you will use to plan, write and edit your essay (allow a few minutes at the end for checking your work).

Plan your essay (you can type directly into the text box or use the erasable booklet).
- Make short notes on your main ideas.
- Sequence your ideas: organise them into a logical order.
- Check your plan against the essay question and make sure the ideas are relevant.

2 WHILE WRITING

Present your main points using your plan. Make sure you argue them clearly and with convincing evidence and examples to support your points.

Always check what you are writing. Type your ideas quickly, but regularly check your content against your plan and the task requirements.

Include everything the essay task asks for. Make sure you focus on the topic and give relevant examples and ideas.

Don't make big changes while you write. You won't have time to start again and complete the task. If you develop better ideas while you're writing, stick with your plan but fit the new ideas in only if you can do so smoothly.

Check the word count and timer regularly.

Use a variety of sentence structures, but stick to grammar which you know you can use correctly, to make fewer mistakes.

3 AFTER WRITING

Read your finished essay and think about how effective it is.
- Is the content relevant and does it answer the essay question?
- Are the ideas clear for the reader?
- Are the introduction, the main ideas in the body, and the conclusion presented in separate paragraphs?
- Is the conclusion clear?
- Have you used a variety of words and phrases to avoid repetition?
- Are the connections between sentences and paragraphs clearly signposted using suitable words and expressions?
- Could the choice of words or phrases be improved?
- Is the total word count between 200 and 300 words?
- Have you spent time checking your grammar, spelling and punctuation?

Make sure you ...

✓ **use paragraphs in an appropriate essay structure.**
  ✗ Don't use bullet points or headings in your essay.

✓ **make sure you write enough!**
  ✗ Don't write fewer than 200 words. Your essay could be too short, which might affect your score.

✓ **only write between 200–300 words.**
  ✗ Don't write too much. There are no extra points for long essays and this may affect your score.

✓ **use language suitable for an academic context.**
  ✗ Don't include casual language or slang, which are not appropriate for writing essays.

✓ **follow a logical structure and link your ideas and arguments clearly.**
  ✗ Don't pack too many ideas into one paragraph.

✓ **answer the task question directly.**
  ✗ Don't give a memorised response, or you risk scoring zero, even if your grammar and spelling are perfect.

✓ **try to use synonyms and paraphrasing to avoid repetition.**
  ✗ Don't repeat or overuse the same words.

 Watch the *Write essay: common mistakes* video for more tips and guidance on this task.

Practice ❯ Write essay

Here is a sample *Write essay* question for you to practise.

 Practise *Write essay 2* here, if you want to try *Write essay* without a time limit. Think about the strategies on pages 56–57. Then follow the task instructions and write your essay.

 Find *Write essay 2* in the **Online Question Bank** to complete it under timed conditions.

> **You will have 20 minutes to plan, write and revise an essay about the topic below. Your response will be judged on how well you develop a position, organize your ideas, present supporting details, and control the elements of standard written English. You should write 200–300 words.**
>
> Some people believe that tertiary education should focus mainly on preparation for the workplace. Others see it as a broader preparation for life. Explain where your opinion lies between these points of view, giving reasons and/or examples as justification.
>
> _____
> _____
> _____
> _____
> _____
> _____
> _____
> _____
> _____
> _____
> _____

❯ Reflecting on your practice

1 Use the checklist below to decide what you did well and what you need to practise more. Set time aside to work on each area that you want to improve.

Write essay text checklist

I read the essay question carefully and I understood what to do.	○	I paid attention to the timer and allowed time at the end to check my essay.	○
I planned my essay.	○	I included an introduction, body paragraphs and a conclusion.	○
I used my plan to write my essay.	○		
I paid attention to word count while writing.	○	I used a variety of vocabulary and grammatical structures.	○
I used suitable linking words to connect my ideas.	○	I checked that my essay content was relevant.	○

2 Read a model answer for this task in the Answer Key. Compare it to your own response. What are the differences? Are you happy with your response? What could you improve?

 For more practice with *Write essay* tasks, go to the **Online Question Bank**.

 Go to the **Online Resources** for extra study tools. See the Writing Resources for a *Write essay Worksheet*, as well as *Useful Language for Writing* and *How to Structure Academic Writing for Essays*.

Building confidence: Writing

› Effective writing skills

To achieve your test score goals, you may need to improve your general writing skills in English (including grammar, spelling vocabulary and written discourse), as well as become familiar with the task types.

WELL-ORGANISED WRITING
How well your writing is organised can have an huge effect on how effectively you convey your ideas.

Plan your piece of writing carefully. Make sure you spend enough time planning. This will help you to organise your key points and decide how you will link them.

Make sure you clearly identify your writing goal. *Write essay* tasks require you to address a specific question and you may need to give an opinion, compare and contrast, suggest a solution, agree or disagree, argue for or against, or discuss advantages and disadvantages. The exact purpose should be clear from the question. In *Summarize written text* tasks, you need to be able to comprehend, analyse and combine information from the recording or text to create an organised summary.

Identify the general topic and specific requirements of each task. For example, in the *Write essay* question *Do you think everyone will use driverless cars in future?*, the general topic is '*driverless cars*' but test takers cannot simply describe these cars. They must address the specific goal of the task, which is explaining whether everyone will use these cars in future. Read the question carefully and make sure you understand its demands. Practise developing outlines for essay topics and review each one to see if it addresses the topic requirements.

Structure your writing carefully. In *Write Essay*, for example, begin with a clear, direct and concise introduction. Then use paragraphs that begin with a topic sentence (which clearly communicates the main idea of the paragraph) and finish with a summary.

Use signposting words. Using words such as *first*, *second* and *finally* can help make your writing clearer and more logical.

Learn how to write clear and concise summaries and conclusions. Summarising using the main points, and ideas from the text (but using different words), is a skill to master and is essential to *Summarise written text* tasks. Study examples of academic texts online, to build your familiarity with typical written conclusions.

USE AND CONTROL OF LANGUAGE
How you use language and apply grammar in your writing can help you to express your ideas clearly.

Use precise language. Work with synonyms and make sure you understand any small differences in meaning. Choosing precise words will help you better communicate your intended meaning. For example, in the phrase *good business*, 'good' could mean many things, such as 'innovative', 'ethical' or 'profitable'. Be as specific as possible.

Use grammar to develop your writing style. Study specific structures (such as subordinate clauses and the use of conjunctions) and apply them to combine and contrast ideas effectively within your sentences. This is especially useful for *Summarise written text* tasks, where you can only write one sentence. Look at how cause and effect is expressed in sentences that you read. Try to apply these structures to your own writing.

Paraphrase what you have read effectively. Paraphrasing (putting what you read into your own words) is an essential skill in advanced or academic writing, especially in *Summarise written text* tasks. Practise paraphrasing sentences and texts, then compare your text with the original one to check you have kept the correct meaning.

Use your vocabulary skills to shorten or lengthen your work. If you have run out of ideas, but are under the word limit, try using different expressions, or adding examples and details to support your explanations. If you have written too much, reduce the length by using more concise terms.

Link points together explicitly. Look for useful phrases and expressions you can use when writing (such as signposting and linking phrases) to combine ideas and make the content of your writing flow smoothly. For example, *This is caused by ... An example of this problem is ...* or *A solution for this could be ...* help bring together different ideas.

CHECKING YOUR CONTENT
Errors can make it difficult to read something, so take time to proofread your work.

Take care with spelling. Correct spelling makes written work easier to read. Remember to check that your spelling is correct while you are writing, and double-check it at the end. Also make sure you are following the same spelling conventions within any one piece of writing (e.g. American, British or Australian English, etc.).

Take care with punctuation. Using correct punctuation in your writing will help the reader to follow you easily.

Make sure you are precise, clear and concise. You will need to express yourself clearly and keep to word limits. The question tells you how many words to write and the counter how many words you have written.

Be aware of your common spelling errors. Make a list of all the words you spell incorrectly to help you identify which spelling errors you repeat. Pay particular attention to your spelling of those words when proofreading your writing.

Check your writing for repetition. You should try to avoid making the same points repeatedly.

Make sure your content addresses the topic and question. Check that the details, examples and explanations you have used to support your ideas are appropriate.

 For more information and tips for improving writing skills, go to to *Useful Language for Writing*, *How to Structure Academic Writing* and *Improving Writing Skills* in the **Online Resources**

› Effective writing skills checklist

Think about your writing skills in English. Use this checklist to identify your strengths and areas where you could improve.

BUILDING CONFIDENCE: WRITING

WELL-ORGANISED WRITING	I feel confident	I could practise more	I need to improve my skills
I am able to identify the purpose of a piece of writing (such as to inform or persuade the reader).	○	○	○
I understand the difference between the task topic and the task requirements.	○	○	○
I can pinpoint the goals I need to achieve in a writing task and focus my writing on them.	○	○	○
I can plan my writing effectively to arrange the ideas or information a way that is logical and easy to follow.	○	○	○
I can arrange the sections, paragraphs and information in a logical order, using the beginning, middle and end of it for different purposes.	○	○	○
I can follow standard writing conventions for writing an essay or summarising something I read.	○	○	○
I can present my key points in the first paragraph in a few concise sentences.	○	○	○
I have the language and tools to write a clear summary or conclusion that brings my ideas together.	○	○	○
I can use signposting words in my writing to show it is coherent and well organised.	○	○	○

USE AND CONTROL OF LANGUAGE	✔	✔	✔
I have a wide range of vocabulary ready to use in my writing and can apply it to familiar and unfamiliar topics.	○	○	○
I can use appropriate words and phrases to express my intended meaning.	○	○	○
I can describe similar ideas in more than one way.	○	○	○
I have developed specific grammar skills that will help me to express multiple ideas in a concise way.	○	○	○
I understand the subtle differences between some key words or phrases in English and how to apply them.	○	○	○
I can use language that is appropriate to the context at hand.	○	○	○
I can use common punctuation conventions.	○	○	○
I can spell most words correctly.	○	○	○
I can apply varied grammar to construct effective sentences and build connections between ideas.	○	○	○
I can use specific language functions to link my ideas together, so they are understandable to the reader.	○	○	○
I can cut text appropriately or use my language skills to expand on ideas, in order to keep within word limits.	○	○	○
I know how to check my writing and make sure I have addressed the topic and the task requirements.	○	○	○

❯ Building blocks for test confidence

1 READING SKILLS FOR WRITING
Improving your general reading skills can improve your written English skills for PTE Academic tasks, where you have to respond to what you read. By fine tuning your reading skills, you can:
- identify key points necessary for constructing an appropriate written response;
- learn to balance reading and writing time during *Summarize written text* tasks;
- pick up useful words, phrases and expressions to use when writing;
- understand concrete information as well as information that is not explicitly described.

2 NOTETAKING
Effective notetaking can help you structure your writing and avoid losing track of the ideas you want to express. It can be useful for gathering ideas together when under a time limit. It can also help you to organise your thoughts and get ready to start writing.

In *Write essay* tasks, notetaking can help you to pinpoint key points in the question and identify your goals for writing, as well as prepare a writing plan. In *Summarize written text* tasks, taking notes can help you to pull out ideas that you need to include in your summary.

3 TIME MANAGEMENT
Each writing task has a specific time limit. How you balance your time between planning, writing and proofreading can affect your ability to complete the task. For example, in *Write essay* tasks you could decide to spend two minutes planning what you will write, fifteen minutes writing and then three minutes checking your work.

For *Summarize written text* tasks, time yourself taking one minute to skim for the main idea, two minutes to read carefully and take notes, five minutes writing a one-sentence summary and two minutes checking your writing. Practising this repeatedly can help you develop awareness of how long each step takes.

Leaving time for proofreading is essential. Remember that you won't have a spelling and grammar tool in the test, so its helpful to be aware of the common errors you make when writing (with spelling, punctuation and grammar) and check for them in your writing.

4 CRITICAL THINKING SKILLS
Thinking critically when writing means gathering, analysing and evaluating ideas and evidence. Practise doing this by reading example questions for *Write essay* tasks. If you need to propose a solution, consider a number of possible solutions and compare. If you need to describe advantages, write as many as possible before evaluating which is the most important.

❯ Keys for confidence

Take every opportunity you have to improve your written English. Make use of apps, websites, or emails etc. to practise writing in different situations.

Practise free writing to improve creativity. Don't let the number of mistakes you make affect your confidence. Decide on a simple topic and write as much as possible about it without worrying about spelling or punctuation. This is sometimes called 'free writing' and it has been proven to build confidence and to help people write more quickly and more creatively.

Challenge yourself to write about an unfamiliar topic each week. Writing about new subjects will help you meet the demands of the exam.

Always review your writing. This will show you what you do well, and will help you spot areas to improve. Compare previous and newer pieces of writing to monitor your progress.

Part 2 | Reading

PART 2: READING

Overview

Part 2 of PTE Academic is focused on reading. This part tests your ability to understand authentic written English in an academic environment.

Part 2 lasts **approximately 32–41 minutes**, which is the total time for all the reading tasks. The exact time within this range depends on the combination of task types you receive.

There are **five reading task types**, and you will complete **15–20 tasks** in total in this part of the test.

Part 2 (Reading)

Task type	Number of tasks	Task description	Skills assessed	Text length
Reading & writing: Fill in the blanks	5–6	A text appears on screen with several blanks (gaps). Select the correct word to fill each blank from a drop-down list.	Reading and writing	100–200 words
Multiple-choice, choose multiple answers	2–3	After reading a text, answer a multiple-choice question on its content or tone by selecting more than one correct response to a question.	Reading	Up to 300 words
Re-order paragraphs	2–3	Several text boxes appear on screen in random order. Put the text boxes in the correct order to form a paragraph.	Reading	Up to 125 words
Reading: Fill in the blanks	4–5	A text appears on screen with several blanks. Drag words from a box to fill each blank.	Reading	Up to 100 words
Multiple-choice, choose single answer	2–3	After reading a text, answer a multiple-choice question on its content or tone by selecting one correct response.	Reading	Up to 125 words

What is assessed in the Reading Sections

PTE Academic assesses a range of reading skills in this part of the test.

- Identifying the main topic
- Recognising supporting points and examples
- Understanding a wide range of academic vocabulary
- Identifying a writer's purpose, tone, attitude and opinion
- Following a sequence of events or points
- Understanding relationships between different parts of a text
- Classifying and categorising information
- Inferring the meaning of unfamiliar words
- Comprehending implicit information
- Comprehending concrete and abstract information
- Evaluating the quality and usefulness of information
- Reading efficiently under timed conditions

Reading skills

Reading effectively begins with extensive and varied reading practice. This can help you to develop strategies for identifying important information within a text, as well as helping to prepare you for the kind of authentic academic texts that appear in PTE Academic. The task types in Part 2 involve using real-world reading strategies, such as deducing the meaning of unfamiliar words, extracting the main point of a text or inferring a writer's opinion about a subject.

Developing reading skills starts with understanding short, simple texts, one word or phrase at a time. As our reading skills improve and our vocabulary develops, we can read with greater ease and understand texts about straightforward, factual subjects. The more we read, the easier it becomes. More advanced readers move from straightforward texts to longer texts about more complex and abstract topics. Successful readers develop the ability to understand texts about a variety of subjects outside their fields of interest or specific areas of knowledge.

What to expect in the reading section

Reading tasks feature authentic academic texts about a variety of topics from a range of academic disciplines. You do not need any prior knowledge of the topics presented. The topics have been selected because they are likely to be familiar or unfamiliar to the vast majority of test takers.

All tasks are designed to test reading ability, and one task, *Reading & Writing: Fill in the blanks*, also tests writing skills.

Reading task types

Part 2 begins with *Reading & writing: Fill in the blanks* tasks. For this task type, you need to select the most appropriate word from a drop-down list to fill in each blank and complete the text. This task type assesses comprehension of the text as a whole as well as understanding of grammar, and writing skills such as the ability to select the most appropriate word for a particular context.

Multiple-choice, choose multiple answers tasks and *Multiple-choice, choose single answer* tasks involve reading a passage and then selecting the correct response(s) to a question. For both task types, the correct response relates to the content or tone of the passage. Information necessary for choosing the correct answer(s) may be presented explicitly, or you may need to infer which response(s) are correct based on meaning.

Re-order paragraphs tasks involve restoring the original order of sentences in a paragraph. The sentences appear in textboxes in a random order. You must drag the textboxes and drop them into the correct order. In order to select the correct order, you will need to understand the main ideas of the paragraph and identify the logical sequence of sentences.

Reading: Fill in the blanks tasks involve dragging words from the box and dropping them into gaps in a text. In order to select the correct words, you will need to understand the sentence around the gap and the passage as a whole.

Scoring of reading tasks

You can receive partial credit for four reading tasks types: *Reading & writing: Fill in the blanks, Multiple-choice, choose multiple answers, Re-order paragraphs* and *Reading: Fill in the blanks*. This means that you will receive a score for every correct answer, even if some of the answers given in the task are incorrect. For *Multiple-choice, choose single answer tasks*, a response is either correct or incorrect.

Task type	Overall score	Speaking score	Reading score	Writing score
Reading & writing: Fill in the blanks	✔		✔	
Multiple-choice, choose multiple answers	✔		✔	
Re-order paragraphs	✔		✔	
Reading: Fill in the blanks	✔		✔	✔
Multiple choice, single answer	✔		✔	

Managing the information on screen

During Part 2 of PTE Academic, you will need to select your responses to tasks in a variety of ways.

1. For *Re-order paragraphs* tasks, you need to restore the original order of a paragraph by dragging text boxes into correct order. You can do this in two ways.
   - Click on a text box, hold the mouse button and drag the box to the desired location.
   - Click on a text box, and then click on the left and right arrow buttons to move it across. On the right panel, you can also use the up and down buttons to re-order the boxes.

2. For *Reading: Fill in the blanks* tasks, you see a text with some missing words. You need to drag and drop words across the screen to fill in the gaps within the text. Click on a word to select it, and hold down the mouse button while dragging the word into the gap. If you change your mind, you can remove a word by dragging it back to the box below the passage.

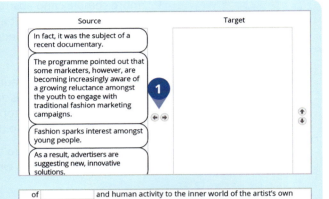

3. For *Reading & writing: Fill in the blanks* tasks, each gap has a button with a drop-down list. Click on the button to reveal the list of options for the gap. Then select the word you think best fills the gap.

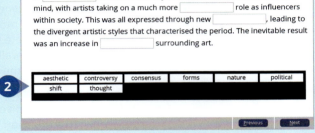

4. For *Multiple-choice, choose multiple answers* and *Multiple-choice, choose single answer* tasks, click the answers you think are correct. If you change your mind, click on the option again to deselect it.

Points to remember: Reading tasks

- For all reading tasks you should read the question carefully. This will help you to understand what to look for in the text and what you need to do to respond correctly.
- It's normally a good idea to try and identify the main idea of a passage before reading it in detail.
- Don't stop reading when you see an unfamiliar word. Information that comes later may help you understand.
- Don't worry if you don't understand every part of a text. It can be possible to complete tasks successfully without understanding every part of a passage.
- Don't rush, but ensure you keep track of your overall time so that you have enough time to complete all of the tasks within the time limit.

Fill in the blanks
Reading and writing

 Length of text: around 100–200 words

Number of blanks: 4–5

Number of options in each blank: 4

Number of these tasks in each test: 5–6

Total time for all reading tasks: 32-41 minutes

Fill in the blanks: reading and writing tests your reading skills, as well as your general grammar and vocabulary knowledge used in writing.

- You will see instructions and a longer text with some blanks. Each one has four options.
- Read the text and choose the best option for each blank.
- Your reading and writing skills are tested.

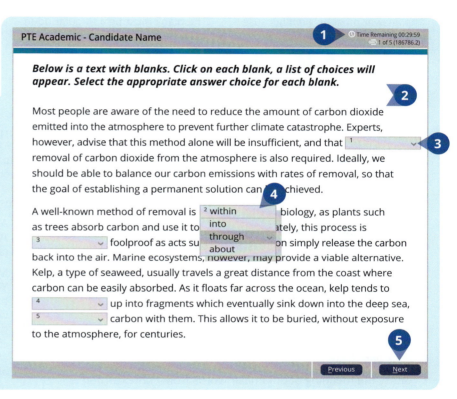

1. The timer shows how much time is left for all the reading tasks in the test.
2. Read the task instructions and then read the text to understand the overall meaning.
3. To fill in a blank, click on the arrow next to it.
4. Then, four options appear in a list. Click on an option to choose it. To change your choice, just click on a different option.
5. Click 'Next' to go to the next question after you have checked your answer.

Skills tested

❯ Reading
- Following a logical or chronological sequence
- Understanding supporting points or examples
- Identifying words and phrases appropriate to the context
- Inferring the meaning of unfamiliar words

❯ Writing
- Using appropriate vocabulary (including academic vocabulary) and collocations
- Making appropriate and accurate grammatical choices

Points to remember: Reading tasks

- *Fill in the blanks: reading* and *Fill in the blanks: reading and writing* tasks look similar. However, *Fill in the blanks: reading* tests your overall understanding of the text, while *Fill in the blanks: reading and writing* tests your grammar or vocabulary choices.

- **The reading section of the test has 15-20 tasks that you need to complete.** When you are satisfied with your response for a task, click 'Next' to move on to the next one.

FILL IN THE BLANKS: READING AND WRITING | 65

Strategies for success ▸ Before the test

There are different ways to fill in each blank. Get into the habit of thinking about these three things.

1. MEANING

Read the sentence with each option in turn. Which one seems to work best in context?

> The fall in net revenue left investors feeling ____
>
> **OPTIONS:**
> ecstatic, glum, idle, dozy

The answer must be *glum* because it wouldn't make sense for the investors to feel ecstatic (happy), idle (lazy) or dozy (tired) about the fall in revenue.

2. GRAMMAR

Is the missing word likely to be a noun, a past tense verb or an adjective?

> There were a ____ of actors on stage
>
> **OPTIONS:**
> various/variety/varied/variants

The blank must be a singular noun because it comes after *a*. The answer is therefore *variety* as it is the only singular noun.

3. COLLOCATIONS

What word often appears with the word before or after the blank?

> He ____ the company from his home a thousand miles away
>
> **OPTIONS:**
> runs, steps, strolls, hikes

The answer must be *runs* because *to run a company* is a common collocation.

❯ Practice tips

Probably the best way to improve your vocabulary is with **lots of reading**.

- Practise by reading short texts from serious books, academic publications, news articles or magazines.
- Pay attention to what each sentence is communicating and the grammar choices that the writer has made. Make sure you recognise the tenses that the writer is using.
- Pay special attention to collocations and fixed phrases. Note that 'pairs' of words are not always right next to each other. There may be other words in between.
- Also learn which prepositions are used after certain adjectives, nouns and verbs (e.g. *pay attention to, be aware of, think about*, etc.).
- Guess the meaning of unfamiliar words from context. Then check the meaning in a dictionary.

Practise deleting key words: verbs, nouns and adjectives from the short texts you find online. Swap texts with someone else and try to guess the missing words. You can include options to choose from (remember to add four options if you use lists).

When you practise reading texts, try to **spend no more than two or three minutes on each one**, to help you get used to working quickly.

❯ Language focus

Expand your knowledge of collocations (words that frequently occur together, such as *carbon emissions*, or *marine ecosystems*).

- An excellent resource for this is the *Pearson Academic Collocations List* (available in the **Online Resources**).
- **Make your own list of collocations.** You can make list according to a topic or a key word. For example, take a word such as *climate* and find words that frequently pair with it, such as *climate catastrophe, climate change, cool climate, tropical climate*, etc. You can also make a list based around a verb (e.g. *provide* an alternative, *provide* a solution) or around an adjective (e.g. *physically active, active effort*).

To expand your vocabulary, **find synonyms** of the word using a thesaurus. Write down examples of how to use the new words. (e.g. do they appear in different collocations?).

Your score for this task

COMMUNICATIVE SKILLS
Listening
Reading ✔
Speaking
Writing ✔

ENABLING SKILLS
Grammar
Oral Fluency
Pronunciation
Spelling
Vocabulary
Written discourse

Look out!

You will get a score of zero if you:
- don't put any words in any blanks.
- choose incorrect answer options for all of the blanks.

 **During the test**

1 FIRST

Read the whole text quickly for overall meaning.
- Don't worry about the blanks yet. Just get a general idea of what the text is about.
- Look for key words that carry meaning.

2 NEXT

Read the text more carefully. At each blank, use the meaning of the text as well as your language knowledge to choose the best option.
- Pay attention to word meaning, collocations and grammar.
- Think about each of the unused options to make sure they're not suitable. Decide why each unused word is incorrect, if you can.
- If you are unsure about a blank, move to the next one. The answer might be clearer when you return to it.
- If you're having trouble using meaning and your grammar or vocabulary knowledge to choose options, then **use your instinct**. Read the full sentence with each option in turn and decide which one feels most comfortable.
- If you don't know how to fill a blank, then guess. Guessing is better than leaving empty blanks.

3 FINALLY

Re-read the text quickly with the completed blanks, to check that the whole text and each sentence makes sense.
Feel free to make changes to your answers, but only if you really think you need to. Otherwise leave them as they are.

Make sure you …

✓ **guess rather than leave any blanks empty.**
  ✗ Don't leave a blank empty, even if you aren't sure of the correct options.

✓ **check all the options.**
  ✗ Don't make a final choice before checking. Sometimes an option can seem correct but after checking the other options, you may realise that another one is a better fit.

✓ **check that your completed text makes sense.**
  ✗ Don't finish before reading the whole text including the words in the blanks.

✓ **keep an eye on the timer so you can complete the remaining parts of the test.**
  ✗ Don't spend too much time on one task.

 Watch the *Fill in the blanks (reading and writing): common mistakes* video for more tips and guidance on this task.

Practice ❯ Fill in the blanks: reading and writing

Here is a sample *Fill in the blanks: reading and writing* task for you to practise.

Practise *Fill in the blanks: reading and writing 2* here if you want to try *Fill in the blanks: reading and writing* without a time limit. Think about the strategies on pages 66–67. Then follow the task instructions.

Find *Fill in the blanks: reading and writing 2* in the **Online Question Bank** to complete it under timed conditions.

Below is a text with blanks. Click on each blank, a list of choices will appear. Select the appropriate answer choice for each blank.

The bond formed between a mother and her baby is a particularly close one. New research has provided some [1]_____ into the mechanisms around this attachment. During interaction, the brain waves of mothers and their babies can coordinate, and recent findings show that the extent to [2]_____ this connection develops is dependent on the mother's emotional state. The more positive emotions the mother expresses, the stronger a connection there seems to be between their brain and their baby's. Babies' brains are extremely adaptable in the early stages of their development, and their experiences during this phase significantly shape their progress. What this may result [3]_____ is more efficient information-sharing between the two, which in turn can lead to higher levels of responsiveness. In other words, babies may be more receptive to learning from mothers who regularly share positive emotions with the baby, [4]_____ enhancing their mental capacity early in life. The scientists further note that their research demonstrates the powerful effect our emotions have on our social connections, but such a connection is yet [5]_____ in other forms of relationships, such as those between siblings, couples and in close friendships.

1 perception / judgement / insight / observation
2 what / that / why / which
3 to / at / in / with
4 thus / besides / despite / when
5 to identify / being identified / to be identified / identified

---

❯ Reflecting on your practice

1 Use the checklist below to decide what you did well and what you need to practise more. Set aside time to work on each area that you want to improve.

Fill in the blanks: reading and writing checklist

I first read the text quickly for overall meaning and could identify the main points.	○	I found reasons why the other options were incorrect.	○
I used my grammar, vocabulary and collocation knowledge to choose the best words for each blank.	○	I guessed if I couldn't work out an answer.	○
I changed my answers if I found a good reason to do so.	○	I checked my answers by re-reading the whole text before finishing.	○

2 Check the answers in the Answer key. Were your answers correct? Try to think about how you could improve.

For more practice with *Fill in the blanks: reading and writing* tasks, go to the **Online Question Bank**.

Go to the **Online Resources** for extra support with *Improving your Reading Skills*.

Multiple choice
Choose multiple answer: reading

Length of text: up to 300 words

Number of correct responses: 2 or more

Number of these tasks in each test: 2–3

Total time for all reading tasks: 32–41 minutes

Multiple-choice, choose multiple answers: reading tests your ability to understand the main ideas, detailed information, purpose, organisation, and inference in a short academic text.

- You will see instructions, a short text and a question with 5–7 options.
- Read the instructions, task question, the options and the text. Then choose at least two options you believe are correct.
- Only your reading skills are tested.

1. The timer shows how much time is left for all the reading tasks in the test.
2. Read the task instructions, the question and the options.
3. Read the text. Choose two or more options that you think are correct. To deselect an option, click on the option again.
4. Click 'Next' to go to the next question after you have checked your answer.

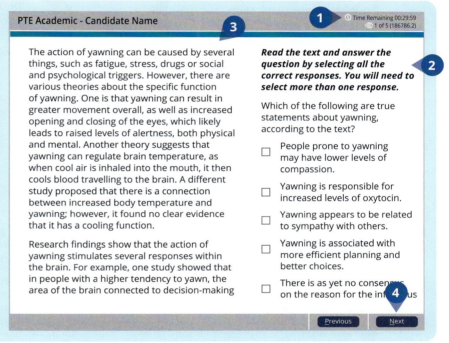

Skills tested

❯ Reading

- Identifying the gist or main ideas
- Identifying supporting points and specific details
- Identifying the writer's purpose and attitude
- Inferring the meaning of ideas or unfamiliar words
- Understanding academic vocabulary
- Comprehending explicit and implicit information
- Classifying and categorising information
- Evaluating the quality and usefulness of texts
- Reading for overall organisation

Points to remember: Reading tasks

- Reading tasks are not timed individually. **You will need to manage your time effectively in this section of the test** in order to complete all the tasks within the overall time for the reading section.
- **The reading section of the test has 15-20 tasks that you need to complete.** When you are satisfied with your response for a task, click 'Next' to move on to the next one.

MULTIPLE-CHOICE, CHOOSE MULTIPLE ANSWERS: READING | **69**

Strategies for success › Before the test

This task tests two key ways of reading.

SKIMMING

AIM: to find the main ideas of the text

With short texts, read the first and last sentence of each paragraph quickly to get the main idea of what they are about.

With longer texts, skim through the introduction and conclusion.

Reading strategies

SCANNING

AIM: to search for specific details in a text (e.g. names, numbers, key words)

You do this without reading every word. Look for key words that relate to the information you are searching for. This is particularly useful for multiple choice tasks where you will often need to find key details quickly.

› Practice tips

Practise by looking at short texts from serious books or magazines. Find some texts (2–5 paragraphs) and then do the following:

- Find ideas in the texts and think about what the relationships are between then. Ask yourself, 'What conclusions can be drawn?'
- Practise locating topic sentences, which can help you to identify the main message. Topic sentences are sometimes the first sentence of a paragraph, and help to introduce the paragraph's main idea.
- Identify cohesive devices. For example, highlight a word like *this* or *it* and then the idea it refers to. Or find a word for an idea that's repeated and then highlight each synonym of that word to follow the idea through the text.

Allow time to practise these tasks while working within a time limit. Try not to spend more than 2–3 minutes on each of these tasks.

Expand your vocabulary by creating lists of words with their synonyms. A thesaurus will help you to find new words with the same or similar meanings. When you learn a new word, record an example of how it's used in context.

Deal **with unfamiliar words** by doing the following.
- Check if the word is actually explained in the text somewhere.
- Try to guess what it means from the context.
- Decide if you really need to understand the word. If not, ignore it.

 ## Your score for this task

COMMUNICATIVE SKILLS
Listening
Reading ✔
Speaking
Writing

ENABLING SKILLS
Grammar
Oral Fluency
Pronunciation
Spelling
Vocabulary
Written discourse

Look out!

You will get a score of zero if you:
- don't choose any options or if you select the wrong options.
- choose more incorrect options than correct options (or if you select all options).

During the test

① FIRST

Read the question carefully. It will tell you what to look for in the text (e.g. if it says, Which of the following purposes …, you will know to read to identify the writer's purpose).

Read the options. Identify key words and think about the differences between the options.

② NEXT

Quickly skim the text to get the general idea. Then read it carefully, according to the purpose you identified from the question.

③ THEN

Ignore any option that seems clearly wrong after reading the text.

Choose options that seem the most likely to be correct.

Try to **decide why your chosen options are correct.**

- If the question is asking about detailed information, find the part of the text that shows your chosen options are correct.
- If the question refers to more general ideas in the text, quickly re-read it to check that your chosen options are correct.
- If you can't find any good evidence for your options, select different options and repeat this process.

- You may see words and phrases in the text that are the same in an option. This doesn't mean this option is correct. Read the text carefully and **make sure you are clear about the meaning** and how it relates to the option.
- **Think about why the options you didn't choose are incorrect.**

Answer the question by clicking on more than one option.

If you're not sure about an option, don't guess. You lose a point for each wrong choice.

Check how much time you have and don't spend too long on one reading task.

④ FINALLY

Read the text again to **check the options you've chosen are correct.**
- Compare each of the other options to the text to check they are incorrect.
- If you change your mind, click on the option again to de-select it.

Make sure you …

✔ **only choose the options you are sure about.**
  ✗ **Don't** select every option. In these tasks, you lose points for choosing incorrect options.

✔ **check your choice with information from the text.**
  ✗ **Don't** decide based on your personal knowledge. Everything you need to know is in the text.

✔ **keep an eye on the timer.**
  ✗ **Don't** spend too much time on one task.

✔ **choose carefully.**
  ✗ **Don't** make a decision based on the length or order of options, or because one option seems odd or different. The questions are very carefully written so that tricks like this won't help you!

✔ **check all the options before making a final choice.**
  ✗ **Don't** choose an option just because the information is very similar to the text. Often the incorrect (as well as correct) options use the same words as the text.

 Watch the *Multiple-choice, choose multiple answers (reading): Common mistakes* video for more tips and guidance on this task.

MULTIPLE-CHOICE, CHOOSE MULTIPLE ANSWERS: READING | **71**

Practice ▸ Multiple-choice, choose multiple answers: reading

Here is a sample *Multiple-choice, choose multiple answers: reading* task for you to practise.

Practise *Multiple-choice, choose multiple answers: reading 2* here, if you want to try *Multiple-choice, choose multiple answers* without a time limit. Think about the strategies on pages 70–71. Then follow the task instructions.

Find *Multiple-choice, choose multiple answers: reading 2* in the **Online Question Bank** to complete it under timed conditions.

Read the text and answer the multiple-choice question by selecting the correct responses. You will need to select more than one response.

When making decisions, we tend to be heavily influenced by the first piece of information that we come across, which we then, often unknowingly, use as a reference or 'anchor' point. Psychologists have learned that once this occurs, we tend to be biased toward processing any other information we obtain based on the anchor, which in turn impacts on our decisions. A simple example is when we choose to purchase an item, such as a computer, and we learn what the typical price for it is. Anything lower than that seems reasonable, and we may subsequently end up paying an amount based on that initial figure, even if it is more than what the computer is really worth.

Research has shown that even seemingly unrelated information can result in us making incorrect estimates. In one study, participants chose random numbers, which then influenced their attempts to answer questions on unrelated topics, like how many African countries were in the UN.

The anchoring effect, also known as focalism, can impact our decisions in a variety of areas. In addition to price estimates, salary negotiations are another prime opportunity for this bias. Studies have shown that the person who makes the initial offer has an advantage as that amount becomes the anchor point for all subsequent discussions. This could work to one's benefit, as starting with an inflated salary request may lead to a higher result than otherwise anticipated.

Nevertheless, we must remain aware of the potential drawbacks of this bias. Medical practitioners, for instance, may be overly influenced by first impressions of a patient or information in their records, which could result in inaccurate diagnoses.

Which of the following points does the writer make about anchoring?
- ☐ Anchoring causes people to exceed their budget.
- ☐ Initial perceptions of a situation can lead to unreliable decision-making.
- ☐ In negotiations, it's best not to be the first person to mention a figure.
- ☐ Focalism is one particular type of anchoring.
- ☐ Anchoring can help find the best price for something.
- ☐ Information in one area can impact on people's accuracy in other areas.

❯ Reflecting on your practice

1. Use the checklist below to decide what you did well and what you need to practise more. Set aside time to work on each area that you want to improve.

Multiple-choice, choose multiple answers: reading checklist

I read the prompt first, then the options and the text.	○	I found relevant information in the text to confirm my chosen responses.	○
I could identify the kind of information to look for from the prompt.	○	I thought of reasons why the other options were incorrect.	○
I identified the main and supporting ideas in the text.	○	I only chose options if I was reasonably sure they were correct.	○
I identified synonyms and paraphrasing rather than just matching words.	○	I checked my answer before moving on.	○

---

2. Check the answers in the Answer key. Were your answers correct? Try to think about how you could improve.

For more practice with *Multiple choice, choose multiple answers: reading*, go to the **Online Question Bank**.

Go to the **Online Resources** for extra support with *Improving your Reading Skills*.

Re-order paragraphs

Length of text: around 50–110 words

Number of text boxes to reorder: 4–5

Number of these tasks in each test: 2–3

Total time for all reading tasks: 32–41 minutes

Re-order paragraphs is a reading task which tests how well you can follow the organisation of an academic text and understand how it is joined together.

- You will see instructions, and two panels. The one on the left has some sentences in the wrong order and the other is empty.
- Drag the sentences to the empty panel, putting them in the right order.
- This task tests your reading skills.

1. The timer shows how much time is left for all the reading tasks in the test.
2. Read the task instructions.
3. Use the arrow buttons between the panels to move boxes between the left and right panels or drag and drop them. You can move the boxes around as much as you like:
   - click on a box to select it, then drag it to the right-hand panel.
   - click on a box to select it, and then click on an arrow button to move it across.
   - double click on a box to make it move to the other panel.
4. You can move the boxes in the right-hand panel (by using the up and down arrow buttons or dragging and dropping the text).
5. Click 'Next' to go to the next question after you have checked your answer.

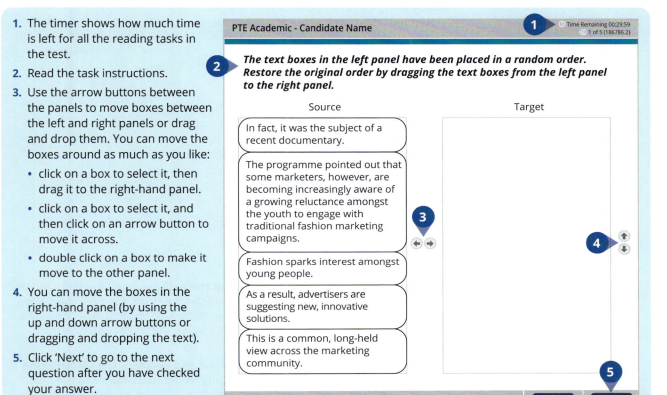

Skills tested

› Reading

- Following a logical or chronological sequence
- Identifying supporting points or examples
- Identifying relationships in the text
- Understanding academic vocabulary
- Inferring the meaning of unfamiliar words
- Comprehending abstract and concrete information

Points to remember: Reading tasks

- The reading texts are designed to test only English. You don't need any special knowledge. **It doesn't matter if you are unfamiliar with the subject.** All the information you need to answer the question is in the text.
- **The reading section of the test has 15-20 tasks that you need to complete.** When you are satisfied with your response for a task, click 'Next' to move on to the next one.

RE-ORDER PARAGRAPHS | 73

Strategies for success ❯ Before the test

Cohesion
Make sure you're familiar with how sentences in a text can link together. Recognising cohesive devices will help you work out the order of the text because they show the relationship between sentences. Here are some examples.

Reference words like *this*, *it*, *the*, *one* and *some* refer to ideas elsewhere in the text.

Different words that are often used for the same idea or thing (e.g. a car might be referred to as *the automobile* and *his new vehicle* in the same text).

Linking words and phrases like *however*, *as a result* and *in fact* which show the relationships between ideas.

Articles that can link to previous ideas: *the* + noun sometimes refer back to where the noun was mentioned before; *a / an* + noun can show that it's the first time the noun is being mentioned.

❯ Practice tips

Practise reading serious texts from websites, textbooks or academic journals. To better understand the connection and flow of sentences, choose a paragraph and do the following:

- **Analyse the first sentence,** asking yourself: 'Why is this sentence before all the others?' Decide whether or not it communicates the main idea of the paragraph it's in, or acts as an introduction to the other sentences.
- Highlight all the words or phrases in the passage that are used for **cohesion**. Decide what each cohesive word or phrase does. Does it refer to another thing or idea in the text? Or does it show the relationship between two ideas?

- **Highlight all the articles** (*a/an* and *the*). Decide why these articles are used. Are they used when a thing is mentioned for the first time? Does the article change when the thing is mentioned again later?
- Look at the text and **decide if the information flows logically** from one sentence to the next. For example, does it follow a sequence such as:
  1 topic
  2 opinion on the topic
  3 detail, reason or ideas
  4 explanation
  5 examples
  Or is does it follow another type of sequence?

Your score for this task

COMMUNICATIVE SKILLS
Listening
Reading ✔
Speaking
Writing

ENABLING SKILLS
Grammar
Oral Fluency
Pronunciation
Spelling
Vocabulary
Written discourse

Look out!
You will get a score of zero if you:
- put all the sentences in an incorrect order.
- don't move anything into the right-hand panel.

» **During the test**

1 FIRST

Skim all the sentences in the text boxes quickly to get an understanding of the topic and purpose of the text. When you have understood the topic and purpose, it will be easier to find a logical order for the ideas.

2 NEXT

Read all the sentences carefully and look for a main topic sentence.
- This will most likely be a general statement about the topic. It is less likely than other sentences to contain reference words (*he*, *this* etc.) or linking words (*however*, *nevertheless* etc.) that refer to anything in another sentence.
- **Move this sentence to the right panel**, at the top. You can re-order the sentences later if you change your mind.
- **Don't worry if some words are unfamiliar.** If you need to know their meanings, try to infer them from the context.

3 THEN

Choose a sentence that follows logically from the first sentence.
- **Identify a logical order** for the remaining sentences.
- **Use language clues** (e.g. cohesion) as well as the meaning of sentences.
- **If you don't know, then guess.** Guessing is better than choosing no options in this task.

4 FINALLY

Read the right-hand panel again to check that it makes sense in the order you've chosen. Change it only if necessary.

Make sure you …

✓ **stick to the key points.**
  ✗ **Don't** try to fit everything in the reading passage into the one-sentence summary.

✓ **clearly summarise the main points.**
  ✗ **Don't** try to make your summary long or too complicated. Remember that a good summary doesn't have to contain a lot of words.

✓ **check the number of words you are writing.**
  ✗ **Don't** use fewer than 5 or more than 75 words.

✓ **only summarise the information presented.**
  ✗ **Don't** add any of your own knowledge, opinion, ideas or evaluation.

✓ **answer the task question directly.**
  ✗ **Don't** give a response you memorised before the test. You will be summarising the wrong information even if the topic is similar.

✓ **use synonyms and paraphrasing, where possible.**
  ✗ **Don't** use exactly the same words as in the text.

 Watch the *Re-order paragraphs: common mistakes* video for more tips and guidance on this task.

Practice 〉 Re-order paragraphs

Here is a sample *Re-order paragraphs* task for you to practise.

 Practise *Re-order paragraphs 2* here if you want to try *Re-order paragraphs* without a time limit. Think about the strategies on pages 74–75. Then follow the task instructions.

 Find *Re-order paragraphs 2* in the **Online Question Bank** to complete it under timed conditions.

The text has been placed in a random order. Restore the original order by numbering the sentences 1-4 (1 for the first sentence, 4 for the last).

The question for many people, though, is how much sleep is enough? ☐

Unfortunately for most people, modern life can make this amount difficult to get. ☐

The amount varies from person to person, but for adults, around eight hours of sleep per night, give or take half an hour or so, is about right. ☐

There is plenty of research showing that a good night's sleep is important for health, in many ways. ☐

〉 Reflecting on your practice

1 Use the checklist below to decide what you did well and what you need to practise more. Set aside time to work on each area that you highlight for improvement.

Re-order paragraphs checklist

First, I read the sentences quickly to get an idea of the topic and purpose of the text.	○	I moved boxes around if I found a good reason to make a change.	○
I identified the first box by finding the one with no references to earlier ideas.	○	I was able to reorganise the boxes into a logical sequence.	○
I found connections between the boxes by identifying language clues (e.g. reference words, articles, linking words/phrases, or words/ expressions with the same or similar meaning).	○	I read the right-hand panel from start to finish to check my answer before finishing.	○
		If I really didn't know the answer, I made the best possible guess.	○

2 Check the answers in the Answer key. Were your answers correct? Try to think about how you could improve.

For more practice with *Re-order paragraphs*, go to the **Online Question Bank**.

 Go to the **Online Resources** for extra support with *Improving your Reading Skills*.

Fill in the blanks
Reading

Length of text: around 40–80 words

Number of blanks: 3–5

Number of these tasks in each test: 4–5

Total time for all reading tasks: 32–41 minutes

In *Fill in the blanks: reading* tasks, you show your overall understanding of a text by dragging and dropping words into blank spaces.

- You will see instructions, a short text with blank spaces and a box containing some words.
- Read the text and drag the words into the correct blank.
- Only your reading skills are tested.

1. A timer shows how much time is left for all the reading tasks in the test.
2. Read the instructions and then read the text to understand its overall meaning.
3. Drag words to the blanks in the text that you think are best. Click on a word to choose it. Then, drag it to the blank in which you want to put it.
   - You can remove a word from a blank by dragging it back to the box.
   - You can drag a word from one blank to another.
   - There are more words than blanks.
4. Click 'Next' to go to the next question after you have checked your answers.

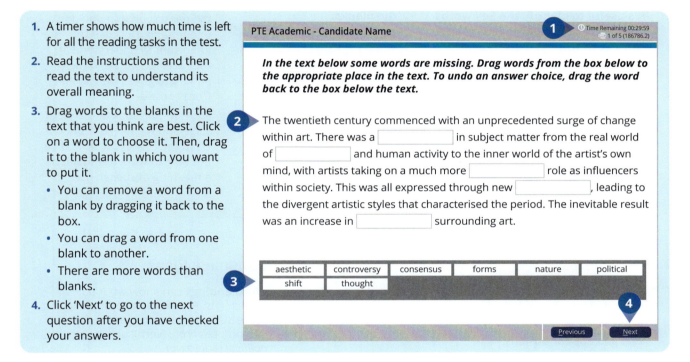

Skills tested

❯ Reading

- Identifying the topic, theme, gist or main ideas
- Identifying supporting points or examples
- Understanding academic vocabulary
- Inferring the meaning of unfamiliar words
- Finding relationships between ideas
- Making inferences from the information in the text
- Comprehending explicit and implicit information
- Classifying and categorising information
- Following a logical or chronological sequence
- Reading a text under timed conditions

Points to remember: Reading tasks

- *Fill in the blanks: reading* and *Fill in the blanks: reading and writing* tasks look similar. However, *Fill in the blanks: reading* tests your overall understanding of the text, while *Fill in the blanks: reading and writing* tests your ability to choose appropriate grammar or vocabulary.
- **The reading section of the test has 15-20 tasks that you need to complete.** When you are satisfied with your response for a task, click 'Next' to move on to the next one.

FILL IN THE BLANKS: READING | **77**

Strategies for success › Before the test

Identifying key words
There are lots of ways to identify the missing words in a text.

> The twentieth century commenced with an unprecedented surge of **change** within **art**. There was a _____ in **subject matter** from the real world of _____ and **human activity** to the inner world of the **artist's** own mind, with artists taking on a much more _____ **role** as influencers within **society**.

When you first read the text to understand its general meaning, it's useful to identify the key words. These give particular meaning and context to what you are reading.

Look at the key words in bold next to the blanks. The key words are used in relation to **art** and **artists**: there was a **change**. The artists' **subject matter** (the things they chose to make art about) changed. It used to be about the 'real world' of **human activity** and changed to being about the artist's own mind. Also, their **role** in **society** changed.

Now think about what kind of words could fill the blanks.

The first blank needs a noun and is probably related to the topic of **change**. The second blank also needs a noun and is related to the topic of **human activity**. The third blank needs an adjective (because it follows the word *more* and is related to the topic of the artist's **role**).

Difficult words

There may be some words in the paragraph that you don't understand. Decide if they are important to understand. If they are, read around them and try to guess the meaning from context.

For example, look at the word *surge* and the words around it. From the context, it should be possible to work out that it has a meaning of *sudden rise*.

› Practice tips

Practise by finding a short text and trying to understand the main ideas. Do the following:

- Highlight key words and try to identify the purpose of the text and any conclusions.
- Write a short summary of the text in your own words.
- Delete some key words. These should be 'content' words (nouns, adjectives, important verbs) and not smaller words such as *the*, or *with*. They should be words that are important to the meaning of the sentence.
- Then, think of all the different words that could fit in the blank you created. They need to be words that would make sense and be grammatically correct in that blank.

› Language focus

Word endings can show what part of speech it is. For example, by looking at these suffixes, you can identify the type of word: *celebrate* (verb); *activity* (noun); *political* (adjective).

Expand your vocabulary by practising changing **the form of a word**. Pay attention to the suffixes. For example, *happy* (adjective) → *happiness* → *happily* (adverb).

Increase your vocabulary by identifying **synonyms** of words you already know. Keep a list of words that have a similar meaning.

Your score for this task

COMMUNICATIVE SKILLS
Listening
Reading ✔
Speaking
Writing

ENABLING SKILLS
Grammar
Oral Fluency
Pronunciation
Spelling
Vocabulary
Written discourse

Look out!
You will get a score of zero if you:
- don't put any words in any blanks.
- choose incorrect answer options for all of the blanks.
- don't put any words in any blanks.
- choose incorrect answer options for all of the gaps.

» **During the test**

1 FIRST
Skim the text quickly to get an idea of the topic. Don't worry about the blanks yet. Just try to identify the topic, the key words, and how the ideas progress across the text. Linkers such as *however* and *for this reason* are very useful for this.

2 NEXT
Try to fill the blanks and think about the meaning of the whole text and of each sentence.
Use what you decided about the topic, the main ideas and how the ideas progress across the text.
If you are unsure about a blank, move to the next one. The more blanks you fill, the easier it will be to complete the other ones.

3 THEN
Check your answers and fill in any you missed.
- Check that the word you put in each blank is the correct part of speech (noun, verb, adjective, etc.), and whether it's correctly singular or plural, countable or uncountable, etc.
- Check each of the unused words to make sure they're not suitable. Decide why each of the unused words is incorrect, if you can.

If you're having trouble deciding what to choose, then **use your instinct**: read the full sentence with each unused option in turn and decide which one feels most comfortable.

If you don't know how to fill a blank, then guess. Guessing is better than leaving empty blanks in this task.

4 FINALLY
Re-read the text quickly, with all the blanks filled.
- Check that the whole text makes sense.
- Check each of the three unused words to confirm your choices and make changes if necessary.

Make sure you ...

✓ **fill in all the blanks.**
  ✗ Don't leave a blank empty, even if you aren't sure of the answer. It is better to guess than leave any blanks empty in this task.

✓ **think about grammar when filling the blanks.**
  ✗ Don't ignore grammatical rules (e.g. if a subject is singular, then the verb should be, too).

✓ **pay close attention to what the text is communicating.**
  ✗ Don't decide based on your personal knowledge – check your choice with information from the text.

✓ **check all the options.**
  ✗ Don't make a final choice before checking all other options. Sometimes an option can seem correct, but after checking other options, you may realise that another is a better fit.

✓ **check your completed text**
  ✗ Don't finish before reading the whole text again.

✓ **keep an eye on the timer.**
  ✗ Don't spend too much time on one task.

 Watch the *Fill in the blanks (reading): common mistakes* video for more tips and guidance on this task.

FILL IN THE BLANKS: READING | 79

Practice › Fill in the blanks: reading

Here is a sample *Fill in the blanks: reading* task for you to practise.

 Practise *Fill in the blanks: reading 2* here if you want to try *Fill in the blanks: reading* without a time limit. Think about the strategies on pages 78–79. Then follow the task instructions.

 Find *Fill in the blanks: reading 2* in the **Online Question Bank** to complete it under timed conditions.

In the text below some words are missing. Fill in the blanks with words from the box.

Economics is all about the choices people make and the reasons they make them. Contrary to popular belief, it's not just about choices around _____. It's actually also about _____ such as how to spend leisure time, who should clean the house or where to go on holiday, even if no cash is involved. In other words, it's all about balancing _____ against costs – not just financial costs but costs in terms of time, enjoyment of life and so on.

| benefits | decisions | interests | money | tax | ways |

› Reflecting on your practice

1 Use the checklist below to decide what you did well and what you need to practise more. Set aside time to work on each area that you want to improve.

Fill in the blanks: reading checklist

I could identify the main ideas in the text and how the topic progressed through the text.	○	I found reasons why the un-chosen options were incorrect.	○
I used the meaning of the whole text and whole sentences to help fill the blanks.	○	I guessed if I couldn't work out a word, making sure no blanks were empty.	○
I used grammatical clues to check my choices of words.	○	I checked my answers by re-reading the whole text before finishing.	○
I switched answers around if I found a good reason to make a change.	○		

2 Check the answers in the Answer Key. Were your answers correct? Try to think about how you could improve.

 For more practice with *Fill in the blanks: reading*, go to the **Online Question Bank**.

Go to the **Online Resources** for extra support with *Improving your Reading Skills*.

Multiple choice
Choose single answer: reading

 Length of text: around 70–110 words

Number of correct responses: 1

Number of these tasks in each test: 2–3

Total time for all reading tasks: 32–41 minutes

Multiple-choice, choose single answer: reading tests your ability to understand the main ideas, detailed information, purpose, organisation, and inference in a short academic text.

- You will see instructions, a short text and a question with four answer options.
- Read the question, options and text. Then choose the one response you believe is correct.
- Your reading skills are tested.

1. The timer shows how much time is left for all the reading tasks in the test.
2. Read the task instructions, the question and the options.
3. Read the text. Choose the option that best answers the question.
   - To deselect an option, click on the option again.
   - You can choose a different option by clicking on it at any time.
4. Click 'Next' to go to the next question after you have checked your answer.

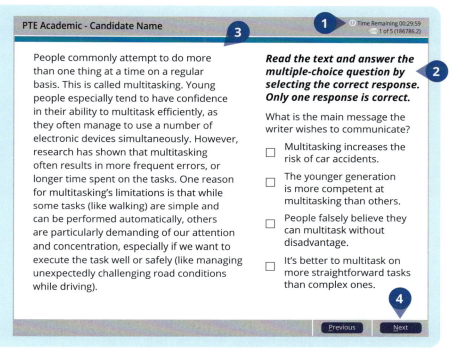

Skills tested

› Reading

- Identifying the gist, main ideas and supporting points
- Identifying specific details or sequences of events
- Identifying the writer's purpose, style and attitude
- Inferring ideas or the meaning of unfamiliar words
- Understanding academic vocabulary
- Making inferences from the information in the text
- Comprehending explicit and implicit information
- Classifying and categorising information
- Evaluating the quality and usefulness of texts
- Reading for overall organisation

Points to remember: Reading tasks

- **Read the instructions and the task question carefully.** The instructions tell you what you need to do and the question indicates the information you are looking for in the text.
- **The reading section of the test has 15-20 tasks that you need to complete.** When you are satisfied with your response for a task, click 'Next' to move on to the next one.

Strategies for success ❯ Before the test

These tasks require you to use comprehension skills and to read and identify one of many things, such as the speaker's purpose, their attitude or opinion. Reading the questions before you read the text can help you decide what information to look for in the text.

Possible task questions	What is the task testing?
What is the central idea of the text? / What is the paragraph about?	Main idea or gist
According to the author, why did … ? / What evidence is given in the text for the writer's conclusion?	Detailed information
What does the writer seek to achieve … ?	Writer's purpose (e.g. to persuade, explain, argue, compare, contrast, present solutions to problems)
What is the relationship between …	Organisation and connections between ideas in the text
What conclusion can be drawn from the text? / What does the writer imply about … ?	Inference
What is the writer's attitude to … ? / Why does the writer use the word *correlation* in the third sentence?	Writer's style, tone, degree of certainty, attitude, etc.

❯ Practice tips

Practise by looking at short texts from serious books or magazines. Find some texts (1–2 paragraphs) and do the following:

- Find out the writers' main point and purpose (e.g. to inform, argue, warn, criticise, describe, persuade, explain, etc.).
- Practise locating topic sentences, which can help you to identify the main message. These are often, but not always the first sentence of a paragraph, and help to introduce the paragraph's main idea.
- Identify cohesive devices. This can help you follow an idea throughout a text. For example, highlight a word like *this* or *it* and then the idea it refers to. Or find an idea that's repeated and highlight the synonyms or phrases used to express it.

Do some online practice tests to get used to working with a time limit. Try to spend no more than 1–2 two minutes on each of these tasks.

❯ Language focus

Develop your vocabulary by looking through texts and highlighting any words you don't know. Practise guessing what they mean from the context. Then check your guesses in a dictionary.

Create lists of words with their synonyms to **expand your vocabulary**. A thesaurus will help you to find new words with the same or similar meanings. When you learn a new word, record an example of how it's used in context.

 ## Your score for this task

COMMUNICATIVE SKILLS	ENABLING SKILLS
Listening	Grammar
Reading ✓	Oral Fluency
Speaking	Pronunciation
Writing	Spelling
	Vocabulary
	Written discourse

Look out!

You will get a score of zero if you:

- don't choose any options or if you choose the wrong options.
- choose more incorrect options than correct options (or if you choose all options).

82 | MULTIPLE-CHOICE, CHOOSE SINGLE ANSWER: READING

› **During the test**

1 FIRST

Read the question carefully. It will tell you what to look for in the text (e.g. if it says, 'What does the writer generally mean …', you will know to read for main ideas).

Read the options. Identify key words and think about the differences between the options.

2 NEXT

Read the text quickly to get the general idea. Then read it more carefully, according to the purpose you identified from the question.

Don't worry if some words are unfamiliar. If you need to know their meaning, try to guess it from the context.

3 THEN

Choose an option that seems the most likely to be correct.

- Ignore any option that seems clearly wrong after reading the text.
- Try to decide why the other options are incorrect as well as why your chosen option is correct. If you can't find any good evidence for an option, select a different one.
- If the question is asking about detailed information, find the part of the text that shows your chosen option is correct.
- If the question refers to more general ideas in the text, quickly re-read it to check that your chosen option is correct.
- You may see words and phrases in the text that are the same in an option. This doesn't mean that this option is correct answer. Read the text carefully and make sure you are clear about the meaning and how it relates to the option.
- If you don't know, guess. In this task, guessing is better than choosing no options. Check how much time you have and don't spend too long on one reading task.

4 FINALLY

Read the text again to check that the option you've chosen is correct. Change it if necessary.

CHOOSE SINGLE ANSWER: READING

Make sure you …

- ✓ **make a guess if you aren't sure of the correct option.**
  ✗ Don't leave this task unanswered. It is better to guess than giveno response.

- ✓ **keep an eye on the timer.**
  ✗ Don't spend too much time on one task.

- ✓ **check your choice with information from the text.**
  ✗ Don't decide based on your personal knowledge. Everything you need to know is in the text.

- ✓ **check all the options before making a final choice.**
  ✗ Don't choose an option just because the language is very similar to the text. Often the incorrect (as well as correct) options use the same words as the text.

- ✓ **choose carefully.**
  ✗ Don't make a decision based on the length or order of options, or because one option seems odd or different. The questions are carefully written so that tricks like this won't help you!

 Watch the *Multiple choice, choose single answer (reading): common mistakes* video for more tips and guidance on this task.

MULTIPLE-CHOICE, CHOOSE SINGLE ANSWER: READING | 83

Practice > Multiple-choice, choose single answer: reading

Here is a sample *Multiple-choice, choose single answer: reading* question for you to practise.

 Practise *Multiple-choice, choose single answer: reading 2* here, if you want to try the task without a time limit. Think about the strategies on pages 82–83. Then follow the task instructions.

 Find *Multiple-choice, choose single answer: reading 2* in the **Online Question Bank** to complete it under timed conditions.

Read the text and answer the multiple-choice question by selecting the correct response. Only one response is correct.

A recent research survey alludes to modifications in the social habits, mediated through smartphone use, of people in emerging economies. The findings reveal that smartphone users generally have more interaction with people of different religious backgrounds, political preferences, income levels and even racial or ethnic groups, compared to those with basic or no mobile phones. However, it remains unclear whether smartphone use directly leads to this increased propensity for social diversity. For instance, it's possible that people with the disposable income to buy and maintain a smartphone often move in different social circles from those without and so would naturally gain exposure to more diverse groups in society.

What can be inferred from this text about smartphone use in emerging economies?
- Smartphones use is increasing only amongst the wealthier.
- The research was more focused on behaviour than explanations.
- Lower socio-economic groups would benefit from free access to smartphones.
- Smartphones are superior to simple mobile phones for socialising.

> Reflecting on your practice

1 Use the checklist below to decide what you did well and what you need to practise more. Set time aside to work on each area that you want to improve.

Multiple-choice, choose single answer: reading **checklist**

I read the question first, then the options and the text.	○	I found relevant information in the text to confirm my chosen response.	○
I could identify the kind of information to look for from the question.	○	I thought of reasons why the other options were incorrect.	○
I identified the main and supporting ideas in the text.	○	I chose an option and made the best possible guess, even if I wasn't sure.	○
I identified synonyms and paraphrasing rather than just matching words.	○	I checked my answer before moving on.	○

2 Check the answer in the Answer key. Was your answer correct? Try to think about how you could improve.

 For more practice with *Multiple-choice, choose single answer: reading*, go to the **Online Question Bank**.

 Go to the **Online Resources** for extra support with *Improving your Reading Skills*.

Building confidence: Reading

› Effective reading skills

To achieve your test score goals, you may need to improve your general reading skills in English, which includes working on some of your enabling skills for reading (vocabulary and grammar) .

READING STRATEGICALLY

There are different strategies you should apply to each task type, in order to read efficiently and achieve the task goals.

Try out different reading styles. We use a range of reading styles in daily life, whether for everyday reading, or for academic and professional purposes. For each specific purpose, we apply different approaches. It is important to practice using active and varied reading strategies, to prepare for reading under timed conditions in the test.

Read for a specific purpose. Before reading a text, make sure you are clear on the task at hand. Are you looking for specific information? Do you need to read in detail to understand the whole text? Or is reading quickly to understand the gist of the text enough?

Practice skimming and scanning. Skimming (reading quickly to get a general overview of the material) and scanning (reading quickly to locate specific information) are key skills for the timed reading tasks in PTE Academic. Find academic texts, set a time limit and practice skimming for overall meaning.

Ask yourself why the text was written. A writer will always have a purpose, for example, to inform or persuade the reader. Identifying a writer's purpose will help you think about the text and understand it.

ANALYSING TEXT STRUCTURE

Being familiar with how academic texts are structured and how writers develop ideas can help you to locate information more easily.

Read different types of academic texts. There are many genres within academic writing: essays, case studies, book reviews, diaries, research proposals and scientific reports. You may not need to write all of them, but it is likely you will need to read many. Read a variety of texts and become familiar with their different styles and the way they are organised.

Understand how texts are organised. Being able to quickly identify titles, subheadings, topic sentences, supporting sentences and opinions can help you locate information more easily. Practise highlighting these different parts when you are reading.

Pay attention to introductions and conclusions. Well written introductions and conclusions will clearly summarise the author's purpose and can be very valuable when reading for gist.

Break down paragraphs where possible. Academic writing will often have well-structured paragraphs. Texts might begin with a topic sentence, then give supporting evidence, and finally make an observation that links back to the overall theme. Focusing on these when reading can help you locate key information more quickly.

SKILLS FOR READING

Improving your general language skills can help you approach academic texts with confidence.

Learn English word roots, prefixes and suffixes, such as *anti-*, *geo-* and *-ness*. You are always likely to encounter unfamiliar vocabulary when reading academic texts. Learning these common parts of language will help you identify the meaning of new words.

Avoid translating new words into your own language when reading. This prevents you from building your vocabulary. Try to learn new words using other English synonyms, which will reinforce your knowledge of synonym.

Expand your knowledge of word order and collocations. Words that are frequently used together are known as collocations, such as *overall aim* or *major advantage*. Keeping a list and learning to recognise collocations in a text can help you to improve your skills for reading tasks such as *Fill in the blanks*.

Practice guessing the meaning of words from context. Highlight all of the words in a text that you don't know and try to guess their meaning from the topic and the words and phrases around them.

For more information and tips for improving reading skills, go to to *Improving Reading Skills* in the **Online Resources**

Effective reading skills checklist

Think about your reading skills in English. Use this checklist to identify your strengths and areas where you could improve.

BUILDING CONFIDENCE: READING

STRATEGIES FOR READING	I feel confident ✔	I could practise more ✔	I need to improve my skills ✔
I can recognise the features, style and focus of a text quickly	●	●	●
I can adapt my reading style to the type of text I am reading	●	●	●
I know how to adapt my reading technique to find the information I am looking for	●	●	●
I understand the difference between reading for gist and reading for specific details	●	●	●
I know how to scan a text for general ideas and skim a text for key details	●	●	●
I can confirm my answer ideas by finding information in the text that supports them	●	●	●
I have practised guessing the answer if I am unsure, based on the context of what I am reading	●	●	●

ANALYSING A TEXT	✔	✔	✔
I know how to identify a topic sentence and use it to understand the main focus of the text	●	●	●
I can locate detailed information or arguments by looking at specific parts of a text, like introductions or conclusions	●	●	●
I know how to use titles, sub-headings and text structure to identify key information	●	●	●
I understand how paraphrasing works and how to use it to identify correct answer options	●	●	●
I can use my grammar and collocations knowledge to identify specific language	●	●	●

READING SKILLS	✔	✔	✔
I can identify the writers purpose in order to look for details or information in the text	●	●	●
I can locate signposting words or phrases that lead to key information in the text	●	●	●
I understand the basics of how words are formed, which helps me to understand unfamiliar words	●	●	●
I am confident in guessing the meaning of unfamiliar words from their context	●	●	●
I am confident I have done enough reading practice to boost my reading skills and vocabulary knowledge	●	●	●
I try to think in English while I read in English, rather than translating to my own language	●	●	●
I recognise that some words can have similar spellings and different meanings	●	●	●
I have practised working with synonyms enough, to be able to recognise words that do have similar meanings	●	●	●

❯ Building blocks for test confidence

1

PRACTISING READING SKILLS

Practising reading authentic texts will make you familiar with the characteristics of academic writing. This will help you read successfully in the test.

Think about what you understand about a text once you have read it quickly. Then ask yourself what you need to know to choose an answer. Identifying gaps in your knowledge will help you look for the key information you need.

Practise identifying certain structures or features of a text. For *Reorder paragraphs* for example, read a text with short passages and identify why certain sentences come before others. Or look for linking words that help tie the section ideas of the text together (e.g. *However*, *In contrast*, or *In addition*).

Improve your general reading skills by reading short texts and summarising the main ideas. Looking at sentence structure, verb patterns and clause structures while you read can help you prepare for understanding text structure in tasks such as *Fill in the blanks* and *Reorder paragraphs*.

2

TAKING NOTES

Taking notes can help during tasks such as *Multiple choice, choose multiple answers* and *choose single answer*. Practise by writing key words from texts and only noting down essential information, such as words you need to remember.

Target specific things when taking notes (e.g. write down the key nouns mentioned in a text). This will help you get ready for *Multiple choice* tasks, when you will need to target information related to answer options. Use abbreviations, such as 'e.g.' to mean 'for example' and symbols, such as '+' to mean 'and'. These will help save time when you are notetaking.

3

TIME MANAGEMENT

During the reading test you should try to perform each task as quickly as possible, while ensuring you are being careful enough to select the correct answer(s).

Don't spend time worrying about the meaning of unfamiliar words. Practise by reading challenging texts without trying to understand word.

Speed reading is a useful skill. Set yourself targets for improving your speed, but remember that reading faster should not mean understanding less. You can also apply skimming or scanning techniques depending on the task at hand.

4

CRITICAL THINKING

Developing critical-thinking skills can help you to analyse texts and complete reading tasks successfully. When reading, ask yourself questions about the relationships between sentences, paragraphs and ideas. This will help you to understand the text as a whole. Approach every text in an objective and critical way. Ask yourself whether the writer is giving facts or opinions. You can distinguish between them by paying attention to the language a writer uses. For example, verbs like *discovered* and *demonstrated* are often used to describe facts, while '*argued*' and '*claimed*' describe opinions.

❯ Keys for confidence

Practice with the right kind of texts. You are likely to encounter topics you aren't familiar with. Build your confidence for reading academic texts by training yourself for the tasks and the test experience.

Focus on strategies for understanding meaning. You are likely to encounter words you don't understand perfectly. Practice using the context of unfamiliar words to help you grasp their general meaning, and also practise reading past words you don't understand to get as much as possible from a text.

Get ready for reading in a busy environment. Get used to blocking out the sounds of other people. Do a lot of practice reading English in a noisy environment such as a café or train station.

Prepare for timed conditions and distractions. Training yourself to concentrate for longer periods of time and to ignore distractions can be helpful. You will need to fully concentrate on each task and be aware of how long you should spend on each one.

Part 3 | Listening

Overview

Part 3 of PTE Academic is focused on listening. It tests your ability to understand authentic spoken English in an academic environment.

Part 3 is **approximately 45–57 minutes**. *Summarize spoken texts* is the only task that is individually timed. There are **two sections** with **eight task types**.

In the first section, you complete **2–3 *Summarize spoken texts* tasks**. These tasks assess listening and writing, as well as grammar, spelling and vocabulary. In the second section, there are **seven task types and 15–22 individual tasks**. These tasks test listening, reading and writing skills.

Part 3 (Listening)

	Task type	Number of tasks	Task description	Skills assessed	Recording length	Time to answer
Section 1	Summarize spoken text	2–3	After listening to a recording, write a summary of 50–70 words.	Listening and writing	60–90 seconds	23–28 minutes
	Multiple-choice, choose multiple answers	2–3	After listening to a recording, answer a multiple-choice question on its content or tone by selecting more than one correct response to a question.	Listening	40–90 seconds	
	Fill in the blanks	2–3	The transcription of a recording appears on screen with several blanks. Type the missing words into the gaps, while listening to the recording.	Listening and writing	30–60 seconds	
	Highlight correct summary	2–3	After listening to a recording, select the paragraph that best summarises the recording.	Listening and writing	30–90 seconds	
	Multiple-choice, choose single answer	2–3	After listening to a recording, answer a multiple-choice question on its content or tone by selecting one correct response.	Listening	30–60 seconds	
	Select missing word	2–3	After listening to a recording, select the missing word or phrase that completes the recording.	Listening	20–70 seconds	
	Highlight incorrect words	2–3	The transcription of a recording appears on screen. While listening to the recording, identify the words in the transcription that differ from what is said.	Listening and writing	15–50 seconds	
	Write from dictation	3–4	After listening to a recording of a sentence, type the sentence.	Listening and writing	3–5 seconds	

What is assessed in the Listening Sections

PTE Academic assesses a range of listening skills in this part of the test.

- Identifying the main topic
- Recognising when a speaker is giving supporting points and examples
- Understanding a wide range of academic vocabulary
- Identifying a speaker's purpose, tone, attitude and opinion
- Following a spoken sequence of events or points
- Recognising when a speaker changes topic
- Classifying and categorising information
- Inferring the meaning of unfamiliar words
- Understanding explicit, implicit, concrete and abstract information
- Evaluating the quality and usefulness of information
- Identifying errors in a transcription and transcribing spoken English
- Understanding variations in tone, speed and accent

Listening skills

Listening effectively involves being able to understand differences in the way speakers pronounce syllables and how words blend together at a natural speed. Identifying key points, understanding the structure of academic lectures and distinguishing between minor points and main arguments are also important. It is often impossible to understand every word someone uses, but it is usually possible to get the main idea.

The development of listening skills starts with being able to follow slow and articulated speech before understanding standard spoken language. After that, we develop the ability to comprehend a wider variety of complex topics and a range of colloquial expressions. Advanced listeners in English, can easily understand the key points in an academic speech or presentation and summarise it effectively in speech or in writing.

What to expect in the listening section

The tasks in Part 3 require different types of responses, including multiple-choice, filling in blanks, highlighting or selecting words, or writing from dictation. You need to be able to summarise, transcribe, highlight and identify key information.

Listening task types

Part 2 begins with 2-3 *Summarize spoken text* tasks. These tasks test your ability to comprehend, analyse and combine information from a lecture. Your response is judged on the quality of your writing and on how well you summarise key points you hear.

Multiple-choice, choose multiple answers, *Multiple-choice, choose single answer*, *Highlight correct summary* and *Select missing word* tasks all involve listening and then making a selection from a number of options.

For *Highlight correct summary* tasks, you must select the correct summary of what you hear, from several options. For *Select missing word* tasks, you must select a word or phrase from a list of options to complete what the speaker says.

In *Fill in the blanks* tasks, you must type single words into gaps within a full transcript of the recording. In *Write from dictation* tasks, you must listen and then write a full sentence. *Highlight incorrect words* tasks require you to listen to a recording while reading the text of what you hear. The text contains a number of words that differ from what you hear which you must click on.

Scoring of listening tasks

You can receive partial credit for *Summarize spoken text, Multiple-choice, choose multiple answers, Fill in the blanks, Write from dictation* and *Highlight incorrect words* tasks. This means that you receive a score for every correct answer, even if not all answers are correct. For *Multiple-choice, choose single answer, Highlight correct summary* and *Select missing word* tasks, a response is either correct or incorrect. As well as contributing to your Listening skill score, Part 3 also assesses enabling skills, as shown in the table below.

Task type	Overall score	Listening score	Writing score	Reading score	Grammar score	Spelling score	Vocabulary score
Summarize spoken text	✔	✔	✔		✔	✔	✔
Multiple-choice, choose multiple answers	✔	✔					
Multiple-choice, choose multiple answers	✔	✔	✔				
Fill in the blanks	✔	✔		✔			
Highlight correct summary	✔	✔					
Multiple-choice, choose single answer	✔	✔					
Select missing word	✔	✔					
Highlight incorrect words	✔	✔		✔			
Write from dictation	✔	✔	✔				

Managing the information on screen

During PTE Academic Part 3, you will need to select your responses to tasks in a variety of ways.

1. For *Summarize spoken text* tasks, you will use a keyboard to type your answers. You will be able to use your mouse to click and highlight text. There are 'Copy', 'Cut' and 'Paste' functions to help you move text around easily. You should monitor the Word Limit counter to ensure you are within the word count for each task. You should write 50–70 words.

2. For *Multiple-choice, choose multiple answers, Multiple-choice, choose single answer, Highlight correct summary* and *Select missing word*, click the answers you think are correct with the left button of the mouse. If you change your mind, left-click on the option again to deselect it.

3. For *Fill in the blanks* tasks, you need to type words into the gaps of a text of the recording. For *Write from dictation*, you need to write the sentence you hear into the box.

4. For *Highlight incorrect word* tasks, you hear a recording and see a text. While listening and reading, click on the words that differ from what the speaker says. If you change your mind, click on the option again to deselect it.

Points to remember: Listening tasks

- You should read the question carefully at the start of each task. Reading the question will tell exactly what you need to do.
- For all listening tasks, you can use the erasable booklet and pen to take notes in order to guide your answers. This is particularly important during *Summarize spoken text* tasks.
- Take notes of key points and main ideas, but do not try to write down everything you hear, as this will prevent you from being able to understand it.
- Concentrate on what you are listening to. Do not allow yourself to be distracted by anything or anyone in the room.
- Do not panic when you encounter an unfamiliar word and do not spend lots of time thinking about its meaning. You may be able to understand the word later in the recording, or you might not need to understand it to complete the task.

Summarize spoken text

Length of recording: 60–90 seconds

Type of recording: audio only, part of a lecture

Number of words required for the summary: 50–70

Time to write summary: 10 minutes

Number of these tasks in each test: 2–3

Summarize spoken text tests how well you can understand the main ideas of a part of a lecture, then how well you can summarise those ideas. Because the summary has to be within strict word limits, you will also have to use grammar very carefully.

- You will see instructions, an audio status box and a box for you to write in.
- Listen to the audio recording.
- Then write a summary of what you heard.
- Your listening and writing skills are tested.

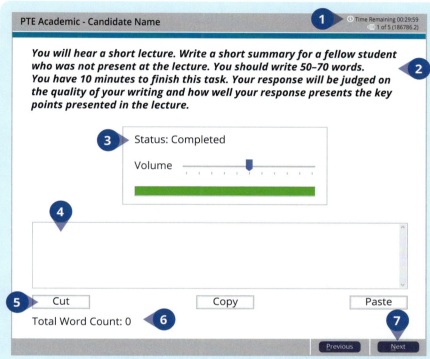

1. The timer shows how much time is left for all the listening tasks in the test.
2. Read the task instructions.
3. The audio status box counts down from 12 seconds to zero, and then the audio will start. Listen to the lecture. You can take notes in your erasable booklet.
4. Type your summary in the box.
5. You can use the 'Cut', 'Copy' and 'Paste' buttons to edit your summary.
6. The 'Total Word Count' shows the number of words in your summary.
7. Click 'Next' to go to the next question after you have checked your answer.

Skills tested

❯ Listening

- Identifying the main ideas and supporting points
- Identifying a speaker's purpose, tone or attitude
- Inferring the meaning of unfamiliar words
- Comprehending explicit and implicit information
- Listening for organisation and connections between information

❯ Writing

- Writing a summary under timed conditions
- Communicating the main points of a lecture in writing
- Organising sentences and paragraphs in a logical way
- Using words and phrases appropriate to the context
- Using accurate grammar, spelling and punctuation

Points to remember: Listening tasks

- Even though you can only listen once to the recordings during listening tasks, **speakers often repeat important information**. Don't worry if you do not understand everything straightaway.
- *Summarize spoken text* is the only task in the listening section which is timed individually. **You will have 10 minutes to write each summary**.

Strategies for success ❯ Before the test

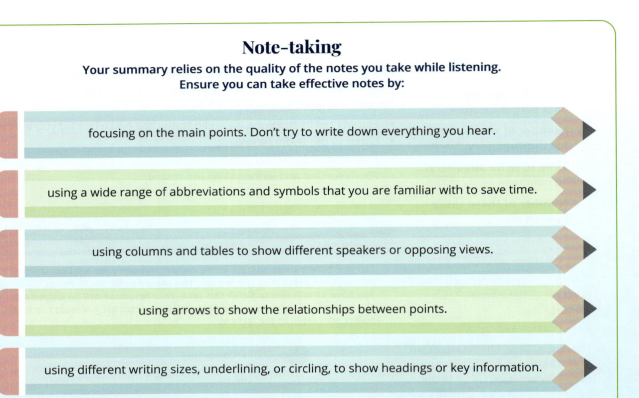

Note-taking
Your summary relies on the quality of the notes you take while listening.
Ensure you can take effective notes by:

- focusing on the main points. Don't try to write down everything you hear.
- using a wide range of abbreviations and symbols that you are familiar with to save time.
- using columns and tables to show different speakers or opposing views.
- using arrows to show the relationships between points.
- using different writing sizes, underlining, or circling, to show headings or key information.

❯ Practice tips

Practise note-taking with the lectures you have found.
- Take a short section of the lecture (around 30 seconds) and take notes on the main idea. Write down key words. Then, stop the lecture and try writing a sentence summarising what you heard.
- Repeat this with the next part of the lecture, and then the next, until you have written a summary of 50–70 words.
- Practise doing this until you can listen to part of a lecture for around 90 seconds without stopping, and then write a summary of what you heard. The summary should take you no more than 10 minutes to write.
- Finally, check your practice summaries carefully. Did you get the right amount of information from the recording? Did you include all the main details in a logical order? Did you use appropriate grammar, vocabulary, punctuation and spelling?

Practise writing simple, clear sentences. This is better in a summary than writing complicated sentences (and the risk of making mistakes is lower). Make sure you are aware of any common mistakes you make (e.g. with word order, punctuation, etc.).

Find examples of lectures on topics you are interested in (you may be able to find some online).
- Listen to short sections of these lectures and identify the main points, along with any supporting details.
- Pay attention to words that the speaker uses to signal a main point or a supporting detail (e.g. *We need to focus on …, The main issue is …, For example …*).

Your score for this task

COMMUNICATIVE SKILLS
Listening ✔
Reading
Speaking
Writing ✔

ENABLING SKILLS
Grammar ✔
Oral Fluency
Pronunciation
Spelling ✔
Vocabulary ✔
Written discourse

Look out!
You will get a score of zero if you:
- write a summary that's too far outside the word limits.
- use all capital letters.
- write about something that isn't relevant to the information in the audio.

SUMMARIZE SPOKEN TEXT

 **During the test**

1 WHILE LISTENING

Take notes as you listen using your erasable booklet.

- Listen for the **main and supporting ideas**, not the minor details.
- **Don't try to write everything you hear.** You will miss important information if you try to write word-for-word.
- **Use abbreviations, symbols and arrows** to help you remember the most important points and indicate how the ideas are connected. Pay attention to the linking devices in the recording (e.g. *because*, *unfortunately*, *so*) as they will indicate the relationships between key points.
- When the recording is finished, start to think about how you will **plan and structure your summary**. Reorganise your ideas quickly if you need to in your notes.

2 WHILE WRITING

Using your notes, **start with an overview sentence** giving the main idea, and then add supporting details.

- Imagine you are writing this summary for someone **who has not heard the recording**.
- Use a range of appropriate grammar structures and vocabulary that you feel confident with. Try to paraphrase the recording rather than use words directly from it.
- **Move parts of the text around** as much as you want using the 'Cut', 'Copy' and 'Paste' buttons.
- Keep editing your summary until you're happy with it. **Check your word count** (it should be 50–70 words).

3 AFTER WRITING

Check the content of your summary.
- Does it contain all the key information?
- Does it have enough supporting detail?
- Does it accurately reflect what you heard?

Adjust your summary so that it fits within the strict **word limit** (50–70 words).

Check the grammar, punctuation and spelling and make corrections where necessary.
- Does each sentence begin with a capital letter and end with a full stop?
- Have you checked for any mistakes with grammar, spelling or punctuation that you often make?

4 FINALLY

Aim to spend a minute at the end to **check your finished summary** to make sure it flows smoothly and logically.

Make sure you …

✓ **Focus on the overall meaning.**
  ✗ Don't be distracted by unfamiliar words. Focusing on words you don't understand might mean you miss more important details.

✓ **stick to the word count.**
  ✗ Don't write fewer than 50 or more than 70 words, or you will lose marks.

✓ **write only about what you heard.**
  ✗ Don't add any of your own knowledge, or ideas. If you go off-topic, you will lose marks.

✓ **stick to the key points.**
  ✗ Don't write every word you hear.

✓ **write clearly, using grammar you are familiar with.**
  ✗ Don't try to write overly complex sentences as you will be more likely to miscommunicate the intended meaning and to make mistakes.

✓ **write a single paragraph with appropriate punctuation.**
  ✗ Don't use bullet points, all capitals or other unusual formatting.

✓ **paraphrase what you heard where possible.**
  ✗ Don't use the exact same words as in the lecture.

 Watch the *Summarize spoken text: common errors* video for more tips and guidance on this task.

Practice › Summarize spoken text

Here is a sample *Summarize spoken text* task for you to practise.

 Practise *Summarize spoken text 2* here if you want to try *Summarize spoken text* without a time limit. Think about the strategies on pages 92–93. Then follow the task instructions and write your summary.

 Find *Summarize spoken text 2* in the **Online Question Bank** to complete it under timed conditions.

🔊 Summarize spoken text 2   **You will hear a short lecture. Write a short summary for a fellow student who was not present at the lecture. You should write 50–70 words.**

You have 10 minutes to finish this task. Your response will be judged on the quality of your writing and how well your response presents the key points presented in the lecture.

_____
_____
_____
_____
_____
_____

› Reflecting on your practice

1. Read your response. Use the checklist below to decide what you did well and what you need to practise more. Set aside time to work on each area that you want to improve.

Summarize spoken text checklist

I could take notes of the main ideas and supporting details.	○	I had enough time to change the word count to fit the limits.	○
I used note-taking techniques (e.g. abbreviations, symbols).	○	I checked my summary for grammar, punctuation and spelling errors.	○
I used my notes to plan my summary.	○	I made sure the summary contained the relevant key information and supporting information.	○
I structured my summary logically and started with an overview.	○	I didn't misrepresent the topic or include irrelevant information.	○
I used grammatical structures accurately.	○	I wrote between 50 and 70 words.	○
I used words from the recording and synonyms where appropriate.	○		

2. Read a model answer for this task in the Answer Key. Compare it to your own response. What are the differences? Are you happy with your response? What could you improve?

 For more practice with *Summarize spoken text* tasks, go to the **Online Question Bank**.

Go to the **Online Resources** for extra support with *Improving your Listening Skills*.

Multiple choice
Choose multiple answer: listening

Length of video or audio: around 50–90 seconds

Number of correct responses: 2 or more

Type of recording: audio or video, part of a lecture or conversation

Number of these tasks in each test: 2–3

Total time for all listening tasks: 45–57 minutes

Multiple-choice, choose multiple answers: listening tests your ability to understand the main ideas, detailed information, purpose, organisation, and inference in a short academic lecture or conversation.

- You will see instructions, an audio status box and a multiple-choice question with 5–7 options to choose from.
- Read the question and options, listen to the recording, then choose at least two options you believe are correct.
- Only your listening skills are tested.

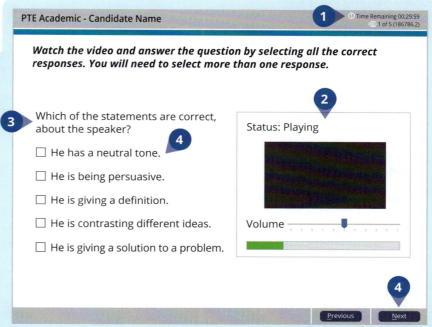

1. The timer shows how much time is left for all the listening tasks in the test.
2. In the audio status box, the status counts down from seven seconds to zero.
3. While it counts down, quickly skim read the question and the options.
4. Choose two or more options to answer the question.
    - To select an option, click on it.
    - To deselect an option, click on the option again.
5. Click 'Next' to go to the next question after you have checked your answer.

Skills tested

❯ Listening

- Identifying the main ideas and supporting points
- Identifying details, opinions, definitions or sequences
- Identifying the speaker's purpose or attitude
- Making inferences from the information heard
- Inferring the meaning of unfamiliar words
- Comprehending explicit and implicit information
- Evaluating the quality and usefulness of texts
- Predicting how a speaker may continue
- Listening for organisation and connections between information

Points to remember: Listening tasks

- **Taking the time to get familiar with each listening task type is important.** You only get to hear the recording once, so make sure you are always ready to listen with a clear goal in mind.
- Listening items (apart from *Summarize spoken text*) are not timed individually. You will have between 45 to 57 minutes for all the listening items. Make sure you practise managing your time effectively.

Strategies for success ▸ Before the test

1 **Make sure you first understand what the topic is.** This will enable you to quickly decide what kind of thing you will hear. For example, if you know that the speaker is talking about a new government programme, it's likely you'll need to listen out for targets, cost, problems, etc. You can also look for topic clues in the task options.

2 **Focus on the bigger picture.** Although this should normally be your priority when listening, with difficult audio tracks it's especially important not to be distracted by less important details. Just listen out for the main ideas. An understanding of the bigger picture will often be enough to answer the question in this task.

4 **Listen to the speaker's tone and intonation.** In *Multiple-choice, choose multiple answer* tasks, you might need to identify the attitude or purpose of a talk. This type of information can often be revealed through not only what a speaker says, but how they say it. A speaker's tone can frequently show whether they are agreeing, disagreeing, questioning, expressing irony, providing evidence, summarising, and so on.

Staying confident while listening

It can be easy to panic when you don't understand a speaker. Practise for this scenario by listening to sources of English which you find challenging. Use the following strategies.

3 **Try to pick out individual words or phrases and reconstruct them after the recording has finished.** For example if you pick out the words *decreased, coffee and Ecuador*, you could guess that coffee sales from Ecuador have decreased.

❯ Practice tips

Find examples of lectures on topics you are interested in (you may be able to find some online). Listen to short sections of these lectures and identify the main points, along with any supporting details.

Practise making statements about the lectures you have found.
- Take a short section of the lecture (around 1 minute) and take notes on the **speaker's main ideas**. Write down key words and use your own abbreviations or symbols. Then, stop the lecture and try writing a sentence summarising what you heard.
- Repeat this with another part of the lecture. However, this time, take notes on the **speaker's intention or purpose**.
- Try to write some more statements about the lecture. This could be about **the organisation and connection of ideas, detailed information, purpose, tone,** etc. Listen to the lecture again and check your statements. Is there anything you can change to make them better or more accurate?

Try to find transcripts of the lectures (some universities have them).
- Go through them and identify the main points of the talk, any examples or evidence referred to and any opposing arguments. Highlight the **signal words** that indicate them (e.g. *We need to focus on … , The issue here is … , What we've discovered is … , For instance, To illustrate, On the contrary*, etc.). Then listen for them in the audio or video.
- Highlight any unfamiliar words in the transcript and **guess their meaning** from the words around them. Check your guess in a dictionary.

Create lists of words with their synonyms to **expand your vocabulary**. A thesaurus will help you to find new words with the same or similar meanings. When you learn a new word, record an example of how it's used in context.

Your score for this task

COMMUNICATIVE SKILLS
Listening ✔
Reading
Speaking
Writing

ENABLING SKILLS
Grammar
Oral Fluency
Pronunciation
Spelling
Vocabulary
Written discourse

Look out!

You will get a score of zero if you:
- don't choose any options.
- choose more incorrect options than correct options (e.g. if you choose all the options).

 **During the test**

1 BEFORE LISTENING

Get your pen and erasable booklet ready.
Read the question carefully. It will tell you what type of information to listen for (e.g. main ideas, detailed information, inferences, speaker's purpose or attitude, etc.). If it says, 'How does the speaker link … ', you will know to listen for relationships between ideas.
Look at the options very quickly. Just identify key words – that's all you'll have time for.

2 WHILE LISTENING

Listen carefully to the recording, keeping in mind the purpose for listening that you identified from the prompt.
- **Take notes as you listen** using your erasable booklet and pen. Use abbreviations, symbols and arrows to note the most important points and how they are connected.
- Listen for **meaning and the flow of ideas**. Don't worry if you miss or don't know some words – keep focusing on what you're hearing.
- Keep looking at the options, if you can. Be careful, because most options will include some information that you hear, but only some are correct.
- **Keep listening until the end,** even if you think you have already heard the information you need. Sometimes speakers change what they've said or add extra information.

3 AFTER LISTENING

Read the question and the options again. **Eliminate any option that seems clearly wrong** (e.g. if it has incorrect information, or information not given). Then choose from the other options.
Aim to **be clear in your mind about all the options.** Think about why the ones you didn't choose are incorrect, as well as why your chosen options are correct.

You may need to re-read the options and your notes several times before making a choice.
If you're not sure about an option, don't choose it. You lose a point for each incorrect choice, so unlike *Multiple-choice, choose single answer* tasks, don't guess!
Keep an eye on the timer and don't spend too long on one listening item.

4 FINALLY

Refer to your notes again to **check that the options you've chosen are correct.** Change them only if necessary.

CHOOSE MULTIPLE ANSWER: LISTENING

Make sure you …

✓ **only make notes about important information.**
  ✗ Don't try to take notes word for word.

✓ **focus on the overall meaning of what you hear.**
  ✗ Don't be distracted by unfamiliar words. Sometimes, focusing on words you don't understand means you miss important details.

✓ **choose options carefully.**
  ✗ Don't select options you're unsure about: in this task, you lose points for choosing incorrect options.

✓ **decide using the information you hear.**
  ✗ Don't make a decision based on the length or order of options, or because one option seems different.

✓ **listen carefully before making a choice.**
  ✗ Don't decide based on your personal knowledge.

✓ **listen for meaning, not individual words.**
  ✗ Don't simply match words with those you heard. Correct and incorrect options use the same words as in the audio or video.

✓ **check all of the options.**
  ✗ Don't make your final choices before checking all other options carefully.

✓ **keep an eye on the timer.**
  ✗ Don't spend too much time on one task.

 Watch the *Multiple-choice, choose multiple answers (listening): common mistakes* video for more tips and guidance on this task.

MULTIPLE-CHOICE, CHOOSE MULTIPLE ANSWERS: LISTENING | **97**

Practice ❯ Multiple-choice, choose multiple answers: listening

Here is a sample *Multiple-choice, choose multiple answers: listening* task for you to practise.

 Practise *Multiple-choice, choose multiple answers: listening 2* here if you want to try the task without a time limit. Think about the strategies on pages 96–97. Then follow the task instructions.

 Find *Multiple-choice, choose multiple answers: listening 2* in the Online resources to complete it under timed conditions.

🔊 Multiple-choice, choose multiple answers: listening 2   **Listen to the recording and answer the question by selecting all the correct responses. *You will need to select more than one response.***

Which of these sentences about design thinking are likely to be correct, from what the speakers say?

☐ It is a quick way to solve problems.
☐ It works best with smaller companies.
☐ You should listen carefully to customers.
☐ It may be suitable for a software company.
☐ People generally find the process hard work.
☐ It is good to choose one idea and stay with it.

❯ Reflecting on your practice

1 Use the checklist below to decide what you did well and what you need to practise more. Set aside time to work on each area that you want to improve.

Multiple-choice, choose multiple answers: listening checklist

I read the prompt first and could identify what kind of information to listen for.	○	I identified synonyms and paraphrasing rather than matching words.	○
I could find the key words in the options before listening.	○	I found relevant information from the recording/in my notes to support my chosen response.	○
I could take notes of the main ideas and supporting details.	○	I found reasons why the other options were incorrect.	○
I used abbreviations and symbols in my notes to help write the ideas quickly.	○	I only chose options if I was reasonably sure they were correct.	○
I eliminated incorrect options.	○	I checked my answers against my notes/memory before moving on.	○

2 Check the answers in the Answer key. Were your answers correct? Try to think about how you could improve.

 For more practice with *Multiple-choice, choose single answers: listening*, go to the **Online Question Bank**.

 Go to the **Online Resources** for extra support with *Improving your Listening Skills*.

Fill in the blanks
listening and writing

 Length of recording: 30–60 seconds

Number of missing words in the transcript: 4–6

Type of recording: audio only (not video), part of a lecture or conversation

Number of these tasks in each test: 2–3

Total time for all listening tasks: 45–57 minutes

Fill in the blanks: listening and writing tests your ability to write the correct words in blanks while listening to a recording. This may involve reconstructing partially-heard words from your language knowledge and the context.

- You will see a transcript of the audio recording. There will be blanks for you to type into.
- During and/or after listening, type the missing words that you heard into the blanks.
- Your listening and writing skills are tested.

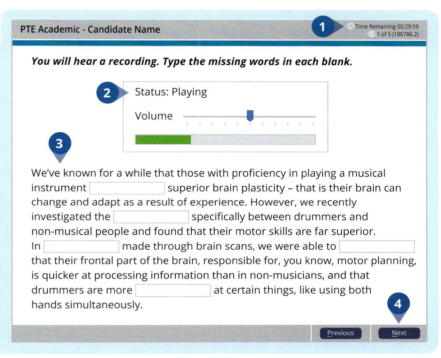

1. The timer shows how much time is left for all the listening tasks in the test.
2. In the audio status box, the status counts down from seven seconds to zero.
3. While it counts down, read as much of the text as you can. The recording will play when the audio status box reaches zero. While listening, you can write the missing words in your erasable booklet if you wish, then type them into the blanks later. You can also type directly into the blanks.
4. Click 'Next' to go to the next question after you have checked your answer.

Skills tested

› Listening
- Identifying words and phrases appropriate to the context
- Recognising the pronunciation of academic vocabulary
- Using context to help identify words

› Writing
- Writing from dictation
- Using words and phrases appropriate to the context
- Using accurate grammar and spelling.

Points to remember: Listening tasks

- During *Fill in the blanks: listening and writing* and *Highlight incorrect words*, you need to read a transcript while listening to the recording. Read the text at the same speed as the speaker is talking. If you get behind, it can make it difficult to complete these tasks successfully.

- Listening items (apart from *Summarize spoken text*) are not timed individually. **You will have between 45 to 57 minutes for all the listening items.** Make sure you practise managing your time effectively across all the tasks.

Strategies for success » Before the test

Practise these skills:

1 Skimming a text to gain a general idea of the topic. You should do this before you listen to help you focus on the words you might hear.

2 Quick note-taking. You might find it easier to type as you listen, but taking notes and completing the blanks at the end is also a good strategy.

3 Paying attention to your spelling. Spelling words correctly could be the difference between getting an answer right or wrong in this task.

4 Reading at the same time as listening. In this task type, you will need to follow the script on screen so you don't get lost or miss any words.

5 Checking your answers at the end.
- You will need to quickly review your work and make sure the words you wrote make sense.
- Using grammar clues to make sure you typed the correct form of the word (e.g. verb tense, noun, adverb or adjective, etc. …).

» Practice tips

Use online listening gap-fill activities to practise choosing grammatically correct words for blanks in texts.

Find some **academic podcasts or lectures** online.
- Listen and pause every 20 seconds. While paused, type the last word you heard, with the spell-checker switched off.
- Play each part again to check that the word you wrote makes sense in the sentence.
- When you have finished, check your spelling in a dictionary.

Practise taking notes while listening and also typing into blanks as you listen. Decide which you're better at, and then use your preferred approach in the test. You will need to type quickly during the test, so practise doing this as much as you can in English.

» Language focus

Create a word bank for yourself and add the new words you learn.
- Add as many forms of the word as you can, such as noun, verb, adjective and adverb, e.g. *distinction* (n), *distinguish* (v), *distinct* (adj).
- Add **synonyms** (words with the same meaning), **antonyms** (words with the opposite meaning) and **collocations** to the collection to expand your vocabulary range. For example, if you add *distinct*, you could also add *indistinct*. Try to make this a daily habit.
- Learn the **spellings** of the new words.
- Practise being able to guess the spelling of unfamiliar words. Write down words you hear in online videos, academic podcasts and lectures. Then check the spelling of these words, in a transcript (if there is one available) or in a dictionary.

 ## Your score for this task

COMMUNICATIVE SKILLS
Listening ✔
Reading
Speaking
Writing ✔

ENABLING SKILLS
Grammar
Oral Fluency
Pronunciation
Spelling
Vocabulary
Written discourse

Look out!

You will get a score of zero if you:
- spell all the words incorrectly.
- write only incorrect words.
- leave all the blanks empty.

 **During the test**

1 BEFORE LISTENING

Read the text quickly to get a general idea of the topic and the ideas that may go in the blanks. This will help you later if you only partially hear one of the words.

Put your cursor in the first blank or get your pen and erasable booklet ready.

2 WHILE LISTENING

Follow the written text by moving the cursor along with the text or by clicking on each blank as you listen, so you don't miss a blank.

Either **write the missing words in your erasable booklet** (and fill the blanks after listening), **or type them directly into the blanks** as you listen.

If you take notes, you might want to use abbreviations for the words (e.g. write *disc* if you hear *discount*).

Don't stop to read what you have typed, or you might lose your place.

If you don't know one of the words, write something to represent its sound – you can go back later.

3 AFTER LISTENING

After the recording stops, if you haven't already typed the words in the blanks, do so now.

Check the words you typed.

- Do they make sense in terms of meaning?
- Do they make sense grammatically (e.g. if the grammar around the blank requires a plural noun, have you written a plural noun)?
- Do they have the correct spelling? (Note: British and American spelling are both OK when used consistently.)

If you didn't hear a word properly or don't know it, **write something that makes sense based on the sounds you heard**.

4 FINALLY

Read the whole text from start to finish, checking that it makes sense with the words you added. Only make changes at this stage if you are sure something is incorrect.

Make sure you …

✔ **check your spelling after listening**
  ✘ Don't worry about spelling while listening and writing.

✔ **listen very carefully.**
  ✘ Don't type a word based just on your own knowledge, opinions, ideas or evaluation. Everything you need is in the audio.

✔ **add something to every blank.**
  ✘ Don't leave any blanks empty. Guessing is better than leaving a blank empty in this task type.

✔ **keep an eye on the timer.**
  ✘ Don't spend too much time on one task.

✔ **check that your answers are grammatically correct.**
  ✘ Don't forget to check that your answers make sense.

 Watch the *Fill in the blanks (listening and writing): common mistakes* video for more tips and guidance on this task.

Practice › Fill in the blanks: listening and writing

Here is a sample *Fill in the blanks: listening and writing* task for you to practise.

 Practise *Fill in the blanks: listening and writing 2* here if you want to try *Fill in the blanks: listening and writing* without a time limit. Think about the strategies on pages 100–101. Then follow the task instructions.

 Find *Fill in the blanks: listening and writing 2* in the **Online Question Bank** resources to complete it under timed conditions.

> 🔊 Fill in the blanks: listening and writing 2   **You will hear a recording. Write the missing words in each blank.**
>
> We use skeletal muscles to move. They're attached to our bones and when they slide together, they _____ our bones in different directions, which allows us to make all sorts of movements like walking, jumping, _____, smiling, and even blinking.
>
> If you don't use a group of muscles for a period of time, they can become weaker, so to _____ this you should exercise regularly. By exercising at a level that you find _____, you strengthen your muscles. When you work hard like this, muscles are slightly damaged and they then _____ and rebuild, becoming stronger.

› Reflecting on your practice

1 Use the checklist below to decide what you did well and what you need to practise more. Set aside time to work on each area that you want to improve.

> **Fill in the blanks: listening and writing checklist**
>
> | | | |
> |---|---|---|
> | I gained a general idea of the topic by reading before listening. | ◯ | I wrote something to represent the sound of the word if I didn't recognise it while listening. | ◯ |
> | I gained a rough sense of the ideas that go in the blanks before listening. | ◯ | I checked the meaning of words. | ◯ |
> | I took notes that I was able to use later. | ◯ | I checked the spelling of words (British or American English). | ◯ |
> | I used note-taking techniques (e.g. abbreviations). | ◯ | I checked that the words fit grammatically in the blanks. | ◯ |
> | I typed directly into the blanks as I listened. | | If I really didn't know an answer, I made the best possible guess. | ◯ |
> | I filled each blank. | ◯ | | |

2 Check the answers in the Answer key. Were your answers correct? Try to think about how you could improve.

 For more practice with *Fill in the blanks: listening and writing* tasks, go to the **Online Question Bank**.

Go to the **Online Resources** for extra support with *Improving your Listening Skills*.

Highlight correct summary

Length of recording: 30–90 seconds

Number of summaries to choose from: 4

Type of recording: audio or video, part of a lecture or conversation

Number of these tasks in each test: 2–3

Total time for all listening tasks: 45–57 minutes

Highlight correct summary tests how well you can identify the most accurate written summary of a part of an academic lecture or conversation.

- You will see instructions, an audio status box and four summaries to choose from.
- After listening to the recording, choose the best summary.
- This task tests your listening and reading skills.

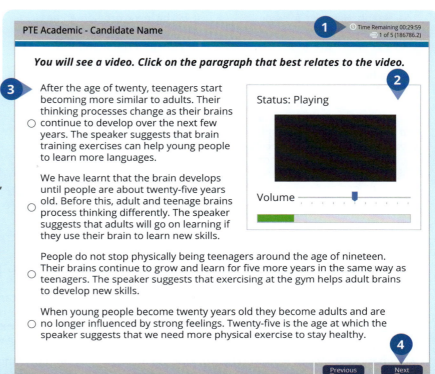

1. The timer shows how much time is left for all the listening tasks in the test.
2. The audio status box counts down from 10 seconds to zero, and then the audio will start. While listening, you can take notes using the Erasable Booklet if you wish.
3. When the audio stops, choose the option that best summarises what you heard, by clicking on it. You can change your answer just by clicking on another one.
4. Click 'Next' to go to the next question after you have checked your answer.

Skills tested

❯ Listening and Reading

- Identifying the gist, topic, main ideas and supporting points
- Identifying the speaker's purpose, tone or attitude
- Inferring the meaning of unfamiliar words
- Classifying and categorising information
- Understanding explicit and implicit information
- Listening for overall organisation and connections between information
- Matching spoken information to written information
- Following a logical or chronological sequence

Points to remember: Listening tasks

- **Be prepared to be flexible with your ideas while you listen.** Sometimes it's easy to think you have identified all the key information after the first part of the recording, but you might change your mind later on. Always listen carefully until the end.
- Listening items (apart from *Summarize spoken text*) are not timed individually. **You will have between 45 to 57 minutes for all the listening items.** Make sure you practice managing your time effectively across all the tasks, to give yourself sufficient time to complete them.

Strategies for success » Before the test

Eliminating false options

In *Highlight correct summary tasks*, it's important to eliminate false options. Practise identifying them by thinking about their common characteristics.

① HAVING A DIFFERENT MEANING

Sometimes whole sentences will directly contradict the original paragraph. However, in some cases it might only be a few words that are wrong. For example, *everyone believes that …* might be an incorrect summary compared to *some people believe that …* Check that the summary correctly represents the subject(s) and object(s); the time scale and sequence of events; the arguments for or against; the proportions and percentages, and so on.

② PRESENTING ADDITIONAL INFORMATION

If a summary mentions details that were not in the recording, it will be incorrect. Sometimes it can be difficult to know whether information was mentioned. Therefore, it's important to take notes while listening. For example, if the summary mentions nuclear and solar power, but you are sure you only heard about nuclear power and have no mention of solar power in your notes, the summary is likely to be incorrect.

③ FOCUSING ONLY ON DETAILS

If a summary fails to mention the main ideas of the recording, and talks only about the supporting points, it is an ineffective summary. For example, if the summary talks only about population growth, when the recording spoke about different effects of urbanisation, it is unlikely to be the correct summary.

» Practice tips

Find some podcasts or lectures (you may find some online) on serious or academic topics.

- Listen to around 30 seconds of the audio, taking notes of the main ideas. Then pause and write a summary sentence of what you heard. Practise this, using longer and longer extracts, until you can listen for 90 seconds and write a longer summary.
- Go back to your summary a few days later. Listen to the lecture again and check your summary. Is there anything you can change to make it better?

Practice reading quickly for general information. Find five paragraphs (approximately 50 words in each) from academic texts. Then try to read each paragraph in 10 seconds, in order to understand its general meaning. Then check your understanding by reading carefully.

» Language focus

Find some transcripts of lectures (some university lectures or serious online sources will have these). **Read short extracts and identify the main points**, along with any supporting details.

- Identify language that introduces a main idea or a supporting detail (e.g. *We need to focus on …* , *The issue here is …* , *What we've discovered is …* , *For instance*, *To illustrate*, *On the contrary*, etc.).
- Listen to the audio while reading the transcript. Notice how the speaker emphasises key words with stress or intonation. Underline these.
- You can also listen without reading. Make notes on what you hear and then check your notes against the transcript to see whether you noted down all the main ideas.

 ## Your score for this task

COMMUNICATIVE SKILLS
Listening ✔
Reading ✔
Speaking
Writing

ENABLING SKILLS
Grammar
Oral Fluency
Pronunciation
Spelling
Vocabulary
Written discourse

Look out!
You will get a score of zero if you:
- don't choose any summary.
- choose an incorrect summary.

 **During the test**

1 BEFORE LISTENING
Skim at least one of the four summaries very quickly, to get a general idea of the topic and main ideas. They will usually be on the same topic as the recording, so you don't have to read them all to understand what the topic is.
Get your pen and erasable booklet ready.

2 WHILE LISTENING
As you listen, **take notes of the main ideas** and supporting details using your erasable booklet and pen. Include, for example, any data used to support an idea or opinion, or any ideas that the speaker implies.

3 AFTER LISTENING
After the recording stops, **eliminate any paragraphs** that:
- contain incorrect information;
- contain information that was not mentioned in the paragraph;
- only focus on details and not the main ideas.

Use your notes to help you, if you made any.

4 FINALLY
Check the remaining option or options against your notes, making sure your final choice accurately contains any **main ideas** and **supporting information** that was mentioned in the recording.

Even if you are not sure which paragraph is the correct summary, **choose the one that best matches** your understanding of the recording. It is better to guess than leave this task unanswered.

Make sure you ...

✓ **use abbreviations, key words, symbols and other note-taking techniques of your own to get the main ideas.**
✗ Don't try to write everything you hear.

✓ **select an answer.**
✗ Don't leave the task unanswered. Guessing is better than not answering if you are unsure.

✓ **choose a summary based on the information you heard.**
✗ Don't choose a summary just because you heard some of the word or ideas.

✓ **listen carefully before deciding what to choose.**
✗ Don't decide based on your own knowledge. Everything you need to know is in the recording.

✓ **listen for meaning, not individual words.**
✗ Don't be distracted by unfamiliar words. Focusing on words you don't understand might mean you miss more important details.

✓ **consider each summary carefully.**
✗ Don't reject a summary just because you think there's a grammar or vocabulary mistake in it. Summaries are carefully written so that they're only incorrect because of the ideas they contain.

✓ **keep an eye on the timer.**
✗ Don't spend too much time on one task.

 Watch the *Highlight correct summary: common mistakes* video for more tips and guidance on this task.

Practice › Highlight correct summary

Here is a sample *Highlight correct summary* task for you to practise.

 Practise *Highlight correct summary 2* here if you want to try *Highlight correct summary* without a time limit. Think about the strategies on pages 104–105. Then follow the task instructions.

 Find *Highlight correct summary 2* in the **Online Question Bank** to complete it under timed conditions.

> 🔊 Highlight correct summary 2 **You will hear a short lecture. Choose the paragraph that best relates to the recording.**
>
> 1. The Mediterranean diet consists mainly of plant-based foods and smaller amounts of fish and meat. It is believed that these foods, combined with regular exercise, can result in improved heart and brain health as well as extended lifespan, although there is the possibility that the people following this kind of diet are generally health-conscious anyway.
>
> 2. There is substantial evidence that the Mediterranean diet, combined with a consistent exercise plan, can offer a number of health benefits such as a longer lifespan and protection against heart disease. This diet favours plant-based foods, and it is recommended that foods containing fats, such as olive oil and fish, shouldn't be used excessively.
>
> 3. Based on the foods typically eaten in countries like Spain and Greece, the Mediterranean diet is considered beneficial with regard to extending one's lifespan and maintaining a healthy heart and brain. Preferred foods include fruits and vegetables, nuts and beans, and various kinds of fish. Meats are included in small amounts, with white meat usually preferred over red meat.
>
> 4. Experts recommend moving towards a Mediterranean diet along with regular exercise in the interest of improving heart health, brain function and generally improving the ageing process. It is thought that by making small changes in a typical diet, such as adding more fish or increasing healthy fats, one can eventually be rewarded with superior health and a longer lifespan.

› Reflecting on your practice

1. Use the checklist below to decide what you did well and what you need to practice more. Set aside time to work on each area that you want to improve.

> **Highlight correct summary checklist**
>
> | | |
> |---|---|
> | I could skim at least one summary and gained a general idea of the topic before listening. ○ | I eliminated summaries because they had missing or incorrect information, or missed out the main ideas from the recording. ○ |
> | I used note-taking techniques (e.g. abbreviations, symbols) while listening AND/OR I could read the summaries while listening and get an idea of which were bad and which were good. ○ | I checked my choice, to make sure it had main ideas as well as supporting information from the recording. ○

 If I really didn't know the answer, I made the best possible guess. ○ |

2. Check the answer in the Answer key. Was your answer correct? Try to think about how you could improve.

 For more practice with *Highlight correct summary* tasks, go to the **Online Question Bank**.

 Go to the **Online Resources** for extra support with *Improving your Listening Skills*.

Multiple choice
Choose single answer: listening

Length of recording:
30–60 seconds

Number of correct responses: 1

Type of recording: audio or video, part of a lecture or conversation

Number of these tasks in each test: 2–3

Total time for all listening tasks: 45–57 minutes

Multiple-choice, choose single answer: listening tests your ability to understand the main ideas, detailed information, purpose, organisation, inference, and/or attitude, etc. of a short academic lecture or conversation

- You will see instructions, an audio status box and a multiple-choice question with four answer options.
- Read the question and answer options, listen to the recording (audio only or video), then choose the response you believe is correct.
- Only your listening skills are tested.

1. The timer shows how much time is left for all the listening tasks in the test.
2. In the audio status box, the status counts down from five seconds to zero.
3. Read the question.
4. Then read the options. The recording will play. While listening, or afterwards, click on <u>one</u> option that best relates to the question. You can change your answer by simply clicking on another one.
5. Click 'Next' to go to the next question after you have checked your answer.

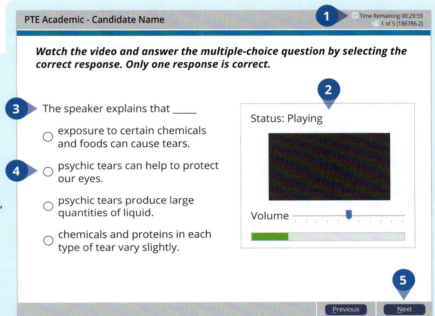

Skills tested
› Listening

- Identifying the gist, topic, theme or main ideas
- Identifying supporting points or examples
- Identifying specific details
- Identifying the speaker's purpose, style or tone
- Making inferences from the information heard
- Evaluating the quality and usefulness of texts
- Inferring the meaning of unfamiliar words
- Understanding explicit and implicit information
- Classifying and categorising information
- Listening for the overall organisation of information

Points to remember: Listening tasks

- **There are always some quick things you can do to get ready to listen**, even if you don't have much time to prepare. Read the listening task questions carefully, and look at anything else that might help you, such as any answer options.
- Listening items (apart from *Summarize spoken text*) are not timed individually. You will have between 45 to 57 minutes for all the listening items. Make sure you practice managing your time effectively across all the tasks.

MULTIPLE-CHOICE, CHOOSE SINGLE ANSWER: LISTENING | 107

Strategies for success » Before the test

Understanding meaning

In *Multiple-choice, choose single answer* tasks, your understanding of vocabulary will often be tested. However, truly understanding a word's meaning can often involve two steps.

Understanding its denotation
This is what will appear in the dictionary. For example, the denotation of *plain* is 'simple or basic in character'.

Understanding a word's connotation
This is the idea or feeling that most people will get from the word. For example, the connotation of *plain* is 'uninteresting and boring'.

When learning new words, make sure to look beyond the first definition. Find the word used in example sentences and look at its synonyms to get a better understanding of how it might be used. If in doubt, ask a proficient speaker.

» Practice tips

Find examples of lectures on topics you are interested in online. Listen to short sections of these lectures and identify the main points, along with any supporting details.

Practise note-taking with the lectures you have found.

- Take a short section of the lecture (around 1 minute) and take notes on the speaker's main ideas. Write down key words and use your own abbreviations or symbols. Then, stop the lecture and try writing a sentence summarising what you heard.
- Repeat this with another part of the lecture. However, this time, take notes on the speaker's intention or purpose.
- Pay attention to words which a speaker uses to communicate an attitude or tone. Make sure you are clear about what feeling or opinion the speaker is trying to show.

» Language focus

Find some transcripts of online audios or videos (some university lectures have them).

- Go through them and identify the main points, any examples or evidence referred to and any opposing arguments. Highlight the signal words that indicate them (e.g. *We need to focus on …* , *The issue here is …* , *What we've discovered is …* , *For instance*, *To illustrate*, *On the contrary*, etc.). Then listen for them in the audio or video.
- Highlight any unfamiliar words in the transcript and guess their meaning from the words around them. Check your guess in a dictionary.

Create lists of words with their synonyms to expand your vocabulary. A thesaurus will help you to find new words with the same or similar meanings. When you learn a new word, record an example of how it's used in context.

 ## Your score for this task

COMMUNICATIVE SKILLS
Listening ✔
Reading
Speaking
Writing

ENABLING SKILLS
Grammar
Oral Fluency
Pronunciation
Spelling
Vocabulary
Written discourse

Look out!
You will get a score of zero if you:
- don't choose any option.
- choose an incorrect option.

108 | MULTIPLE-CHOICE, CHOOSE SINGLE ANSWER: LISTENING

 **During the test**

1 BEFORE LISTENING

Get your pen and erasable booklet ready.
Read the question carefully. It will tell you what type of information to listen for. If it says, 'What does the speaker infer about … ', you will know to listen for something that isn't stated directly in the recording.
Skim the options very quickly. Just identify key words if you can – that's all you'll have time for.

2 WHILE LISTENING

Listen carefully to the recording, keeping in mind the purpose for listening that you identified from the question.
- **Take notes** as you listen using your erasable booklet and pen. Use abbreviations, symbols and arrows.
- **Listen for the main and supporting ideas**, not the minor details.
- **Don't try to write everything you hear.** You will miss important information if you try to write everything word-for-word.

Listen for meaning and the flow of ideas. Don't worry if you miss or don't know individual words – keep listening.
Keep your eyes on the options. Be careful, because most options will include some information from what you hear, but only one is correct.
Keep listening until the end. Sometimes speakers change what they have said or add extra information.

3 AFTER LISTENING

Read the question and the options again.
- **Eliminate any option that seems wrong** (e.g. it has incorrect information, or information not given). Then choose from the other options.
- **Aim to be clear about all the options**. Think about why the ones you didn't choose are incorrect, as well as why your chosen option is correct.

You may need to re-read the options and your notes several times.
- **If you don't know, then guess**. Unlike with *Multiple-choice, choose multiple answers* tasks, you won't lose a point for guessing!
- **Keep an eye on the timer** and don't spend too long on one listening item.

4 FINALLY

Refer to your notes again to **check that the option you've chosen is correct**.

Make sure you …

✓ **only write notes.**
  ✗ Don't write too much. You may miss important information.

✓ **guess, if you don't know the answer.**
  ✗ Don't leave this task unanswered, even if you aren't sure of the correct option.

✓ **make your decision based on the information you hear.**
  ✗ Don't make a decision based on the length or order of options, or because one seems different.

✓ **listen carefully before deciding which option to choose.**
  ✗ Don't decide based on your own knowledge. Everything you need to know is in the recording.

✓ **listen for meaning, not individual words.**
  ✗ Don't simply match words with those you heard. Often the incorrect (as well as correct) options use the same words as in the audio or video.

✓ **focus on the overall meaning.**
  ✗ Don't be distracted by unfamiliar words.

✓ **check all of the options.**
  ✗ Don't make a final choice before checking all other options. Sometimes an option can seem correct because the information is very similar to the recording, but another option may be better.

✓ **keep an eye on the timer.**
  ✗ Don't spend too much time on one task.

 Watch the *Multiple-choice, choose single answer (listening): common mistakes* video for more tips and guidance on this task.

Practice › Multiple-choice, choose single answer: listening

Here is a sample *Multiple-choice, choose single answer: listening* task for you to practise.

Practise *Multiple-choice, choose single answer: listening 2* here if you want to try the task without a time limit. Think about the strategies on pages 108–109. Then follow the task instructions.

Find *Multiple-choice, choose single answer: listening 2* in the **Online Question Bank** to complete it under timed conditions.

🔊 Multiple-choice, choose single answer: listening 2   **Listen to the recording and answer the multiple-choice question by selecting the correct response.** *Only one response is correct.*

Which sentence best summarises the recording?
- ☐ Cybercrime is an important and growing issue for many companies.
- ☐ Companies need to choose the right technicians for their IT security.
- ☐ Companies must give people the technical skills to reduce cybercrime.
- ☐ Making staff follow simple rules can reduce the problem of cybercrime.

› Reflecting on your practice

1. Use the checklist below to decide what you did well and what you need to practice more. Set aside time to work on each area that you want to improve.

Multiple-choice, choose single answers: listening checklist

I read the question first and could identify what kind of information to listen for.	○	I identified synonyms and paraphrasing rather than matching words.	○
If I had time, I tried to find key words in the options before listening.	○	I found relevant information from the recording/in my notes to support my chosen response.	○
I could take notes of the main ideas and supporting details.	○	If I really didn't know the answer, I made the best possible guess.	○
I used abbreviations and symbols in my notes to help write the ideas quickly.	○	I checked my answer against my notes/memory before moving on.	○
I eliminated incorrect options, and understood why they were incorrect.	○		

2. Check the answer in the Answer key. Was your answer correct? Try to think about how you could improve.

For more practice with *Multiple-choice, choose single answer: listening tasks*, go to the **Online Question Bank**.

Go to the **Online Resources** for extra support with *Improving your Listening Skills*.

Select missing word

Length of recording: 20–70 seconds

Number of options to choose from: 3–5

Number of these tasks in each test: 2–3

Type of recording: audio only or video, part of a lecture or conversation

Time limit for all listening tasks: 45–57 minutes

In *Select missing word* tasks, you can use clues from a recording to predict the last word or group of words. This requires an understanding of the overall meaning of the recording.

- You will see instructions, an audio status box and 3–5 answer options.
- Listen to the audio or watch the video, which has the last word or last few words replaced with a beep.
- Then choose the option that best replaces the beep.
- This task tests your listening and reading skills.

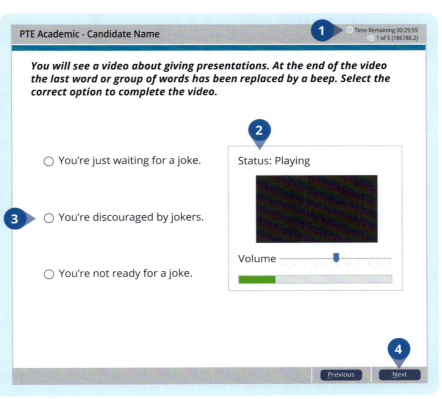

1. The timer shows how much time is left for all the listening tasks in the test.
2. The audio status box will count down from seven seconds to zero, and then the video or audio will start. A bar moves to show you how much time is left on the recording. The last word or phrase is replaced by a beep.
3. Click on the option that completes what you heard.
4. Click 'Next' to go to the next question after you have checked your answer.

Skills tested

❯ Listening

- Identifying a main idea or sequence of ideas
- Identifying words and phrases appropriate to the context
- Understanding academic vocabulary
- Comprehending explicit and implicit information
- Comprehending variations in tone, speed and accent
- Predicting how a speaker may continue
- Forming a conclusion from what a speaker says

Points to remember: Listening tasks

- The audio and video recordings in these tasks are designed to test English only. You don't need any special knowledge. **It doesn't matter if you are unfamiliar with the subject.** All the information you need to complete the task is in the recording.
- Listening items (apart from *Summarize spoken text*) are not timed individually. **You will have between 45 to 57 minutes for all the listening items.**
- Be careful not to click 'Next' too soon. **You can't go back to these tasks to try again.**

SELECT MISSING WORD | 111

Strategies for success ❯ Before the test

Decide whether you want to take notes in this task. Try listening to short audio extracts (30–60 seconds long) with and without note-taking, pausing, and then predicting the next few words. Which way was easier?

1 NOTE-TAKING

Note-taking allows you to list all the main points of the recording, without overlooking any ideas. After the recording ends, you might spot things in your notes that you hadn't realised while listening.

If note-taking:
- only note down key words. You don't need to write down specific details.
- skim the options before and while listening. Then compare the options with your notes after listening.

2 LISTENING AND VISUALISING

Alternatively, just listening might allow you to focus more on how the recording flows towards the missing words.

If just listening:
- try to produce a mental map of what you hear. Visualise the subject and the flow of ideas.
- think about the options while listening, comparing them to what you have visualised.

❯ Practice tips
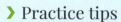

Find some examples of podcasts or lectures (you may find some online) on serious or academic topics. Avoid news sources, as these are not usually similar to what you will hear in the test. Try to find ones with transcripts.

- Look at the transcript and highlight any linking words that introduce examples, evidence or contrasting arguments.
- Listen to the audio and listen for the words you highlighted. Notice how the linking words signal a change in the direction of the talk.

Practise brainstorming vocabulary quickly. First, look for a piece of audio online and read the title. In 30 seconds, brainstorm all the vocabulary you can think of which you might hear in the recording. Then listen and check if any of the words are used.

Generally, it's a good idea to **practise predicting the ideas and vocabulary you will hear** in a piece of audio or in a video. You can also play a short extract of audio, stop it and then predict what you might hear next. Continue playing to check your ideas.

Expand your vocabulary by identifying words from the podcasts or lectures that you want to learn. Check if the speaker uses any synonyms of these words and record them. When you record new words, try to do so in an example sentence, to show the context it's used in.

Your score for this task

COMMUNICATIVE SKILLS
Listening ✔
Reading ✔
Speaking
Writing

ENABLING SKILLS
Grammar
Oral Fluency
Pronunciation
Spelling
Vocabulary
Written discourse

Look out!

You will get a score of zero if you:
- don't choose any option.
- choose an incorrect option.

 **》 During the test**

① BEFORE LISTENING

Read the instructions, as the first sentence mentions the topic. Knowing the topic before listening will help you identify the main ideas more quickly.
Skim the options very quickly, just to get a quick sense of their meaning.

② WHILE LISTENING

Listen carefully for the main points and flow of ideas in the talk – these will help you more than the details in these tasks.
Pay attention to any signal words that might suggest the purpose of the next sentence or sentences. For example, they might give opposite arguments (e.g. *on the other hand*), describe something in detail (e.g. *if we look carefully, …*) or support an opinion (e.g. *because*). This helps you spot if the direction of the talk changes just before the end.
Focus on the options, if you can. Be careful, because most options will relate in some way to the recording, but only one is correct.
Focus as much as possible on the last part of the recording, so that you hear the words immediately surrounding the beep.

③ AFTER LISTENING

Think about what would come next in the recording. Then, read the options carefully.
- **Eliminate any option that seems wrong** (e.g. the information is the opposite of what you expected, or it is on the right topic but says something irrelevant to the rest of the recording).
- **From the remaining options, choose the one that has the closest meaning** to what you expect.
- **Aim to be clear about all the options**. Think about why the ones you didn't choose are incorrect, as well as why your chosen option is correct.
- You may need to **re-read the options (and your notes, if you took any)** several times.
- Even if you are not sure which answer option is correct, **choose one that feels the most suitable**. It is better to guess than leave the task unanswered.

Keep an eye on the timer and don't spend too long on one listening task.

④ FINALLY

Check your memory of the recording and your answer option to make sure everything is consistent.
Click 'Next' to move on quickly to the next task.

Make sure you …

- ✓ **focus on overall meaning.**
  - ✗ Don't focus too much on details or on unfamiliar words.

- ✓ **only note down the main ideas (if you take notes).**
  - ✗ Don't try to take notes word for word. Note-taking isn't essential in this task. Sometimes it's easier just to listen.

- ✓ **focus on meaning, not grammar.**
  - ✗ Don't worry about whether an option is a grammatical fit with the words you heard before the beep. All the options will fit grammatically.

- ✓ **make your decision based on the detail you hear.**
  - ✗ Don't make a decision based on the length or order of options, or because some words in the audio match the ones in the options.

- ✓ **listen carefully for context before choosing an option.**
  - ✗ Don't decide based on your own knowledge. Everything you need to know is in the recording.

- ✓ **check all of the options.**
  - ✗ Don't make your final choices before checking all other options carefully. An option might seem correct because the information is very similar to the text, but another option may be better.

 Watch the *Select missing word: common mistakes* video for more tips and guidance on this task.

SELECT MISSING WORD | 113

Practice › Select missing word

Here is a sample *Select missing word* task for you to practise.

 Practise *Select missing word 2* if you want to try *Select missing word* without a time limit. Think about the strategies on pages 112–113. Then follow the task instructions.

 Find *Select missing word 2* in the **Online Question Bank** resources to complete it under timed conditions.

🔊 **Select missing word 2** You will hear a recording about marketing. At the end of the recording the last word or group of words has been replaced by a beep. Select the correct option to complete the recording.

- ☐ persuading potential customers
- ☐ designing new products
- ☐ research and planning
- ☐ advertising and sales

› Reflecting on your practice

1 Use the checklist below to decide what you did reasonably well and what you need to practise more. Set aside time to work on each area that you want to improve.

Select missing word checklist

I picked up the topic of the recording from the instructions. ○	I eliminated incorrect options. ○
I skimmed the answer options and gained a sense of their meaning. ○	I identified synonyms and paraphrasing rather than matched words. ○
I listened carefully during the recording and followed the flow of ideas. ○	I found reasons why the other options were incorrect. ○
I picked up the signal words showing the purpose of each part of the recording. ○	If I really didn't know the answer, I made the best possible guess. ○
I took useful notes or visualised information while listening. ○	I checked my answer before moving on. ○

2 Check the answer in the Answer key. Was your answer correct? Try to think about how you could improve.

 For more practice with *Select missing word* tasks, go to the **Online Question Bank**.

Go to the **Online Resources** for extra support with *Improving your Listening Skills*.

Highlight incorrect words

Length of recording: around 15–60 seconds

Type of recording: audio only, part of a talk or conversation

Number of incorrect words in transcription: around 5–6

Number of these tasks in each test: 2–3

Time limit for all listening tasks: 45–57 minutes

Highlight incorrect words tests your ability to find differences between words you hear and words you read.

- You will see instructions, an audio status box and a transcript of a recording which has around five or six incorrect words.
- While listening to the audio (or after), click on the incorrect words.
- This task tests your listening and reading skills.

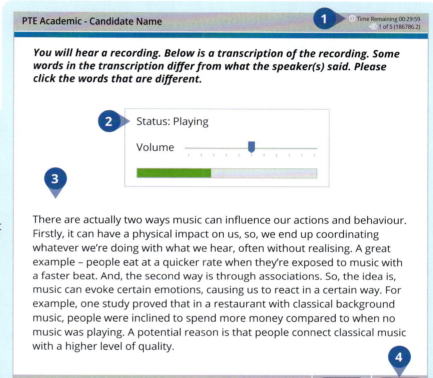

1. A timer shows how much time is left for all the listening tasks in the test.
2. The audio status box will count down from 10 seconds to zero, and then the audio will start.
3. Click on the words in the transcript that are different from the words you hear. Note that only single words, not groups of words, are incorrect.
4. Click 'Next' to go to the next question after you have checked your answer.

Skills tested

❯ Listening and Reading

- Identifying errors in a transcript while listening and reading
- Understanding academic vocabulary
- Reading a text under timed conditions
- Following oral sequencing of information
- Matching spoken text to writing
- Understanding and recognising the relationship between pronunciation and spelling

Points to remember: Listening tasks

- In some tasks you may only need to listen, whereas in others you will need to listen, read and then respond, or listen and then write. **Make sure you know what skills you need to apply** to each task type and practice them.
- Listening items (apart from *Summarize spoken text*) are not timed individually. **You will have between 45 to 57 minutes for all the listening items.** Make sure you practice managing your time effectively across all the tasks, to give yourself sufficient time to complete them

HIGHLIGHT INCORRECT WORDS | 115

Strategies for success › Before the test

Get used to listening to native speakers

Listen to speakers of English who have different accents from places such as New Zealand, Ireland, the USA, and so on. You will come across a variety of accents and dialects in the test, as all of the audio is from authentic sources.

1 Improving your understanding of how different speakers pronounce words can help. For example, some words are pronounced differently in British and American English, such as the word *schedule*, which could sound like:

schedule (BrE)

skedule (AmE)

2 Get used to how speakers often say some groups of words faster than other groups, even in the same sentence. This is natural in English, but means you have to pay careful attention while following the transcripts.

We'veconductedanumberof

3 Pay attention to where word stress is placed differently by speakers from different countries. Try to learn differences like these:

› Practice tips

Find some podcasts on general topics similar to those you may study in school or at university, or academic lectures, that have transcripts. With these:

- Highlight all the key words in a short section of the transcript. Think about how they are pronounced and where the stress is placed within each word. Check this in a dictionary if you like.
- Then play the recording and read the transcript at the same time, checking if you were correct.
- Think about how the meaning of the extract would change if you changed any of the key words.

› Language focus

Create lists of words from the recordings you use, with their synonyms, to **expand your vocabulary**. A thesaurus will help you to find new words with the same or similar meanings.

When you learn a new word, **record which syllable has the stress**. Sometimes it's easier to recognise a word by its stress pattern than by recognising the sounds that make up the word.

Your score for this task

COMMUNICATIVE SKILLS
Listening ✔
Reading ✔
Speaking
Writing

ENABLING SKILLS
Grammar
Oral Fluency
Pronunciation
Spelling
Vocabulary
Written discourse

Look out!

You will get a score of zero if you:
- don't highlight any words.
- highlight as many (or more) correct words as incorrect words (e.g. if you choose all or many of the words in the text).

 › **During the test**

1 BEFORE LISTENING

Skim the transcript quickly to get a general idea of the topic. Don't worry if you don't have time to read every word – just get a sense of the topic and ideas.

Place your cursor at the beginning of the transcript just before the audio status box counter reaches zero, and **get ready to follow the text with the cursor** when the recording begins.

2 WHILE LISTENING

As soon as the recording starts, **follow the words in the transcript as you listen** with the cursor.

When you hear an incorrect word, click on it immediately, while continuing to follow the recording. Remember:
- words are highlighted in yellow when you click on them.
- they remain highlighted in yellow unless you click on them again.
- only single words should be highlighted, not groups of words. Incorrect words do not appear next to each other.

Keep following the speaker so you do not lose your place.

3 AFTER LISTENING

Keep an eye on the timer and don't spend too long on one listening task.

4 FINALLY

Click 'Next' to move on quickly – **checking your answers is not realistic** in these tasks.

Make sure you …

✔ **listen carefully to make your choices.**
   ✗ Don't try to select words just because they look odd or wrong in the transcript, (e.g. unusual or long words).

✔ **keep reading as you listen.**
   ✗ Don't lose track of the speaker, because it will be difficult for you to catch up and you may miss some of the other incorrect words.

✔ **focus on the text while listening.**
   ✗ Don't try to take notes. It's difficult to pay attention to the transcript and erasable booklet at the same time.

✔ **Choose a word only if you are sure it is different from the one you hear.**
   ✗ Don't guess. You will lose points for each incorrect word you choose.

✔ **avoid going back to click on words.**
   ✗ Don't change your mind unless you are sure you have made a mistake.

✔ **choose 5–6 words (but don't guess if you have fewer).**
   ✗ Don't select too many words. You lose a point for each incorrect word. There should be around five or six words to highlight in each task.

✔ **click on 'Next' when the audio has finished.**
   ✗ Don't waste time checking your answers. Words have to be chosen while listening.

 Watch the *Highlight incorrect words: common mistakes* video for more tips and guidance on this task.

Practice 〉 Highlight incorrect words

Here is a sample *Highlight incorrect words* task for you to practise.

Practise *Highlight incorrect words 2* here if you want to try *Highlight incorrect words* without a time limit. Think about the strategies on pages 116–117. Then follow the task instructions.

Find *Highlight incorrect words 2* this task in the **Online Question Bank** to complete it under timed conditions.

> 🔊 Highlight incorrect words 2   **You will hear a recording. Below is a transcription of the recording. Some words in the transcription differ from what the speaker(s) said. Please select the words that are different.**
>
> We've conducted a number of brain imaging studies on patients suffering from chronic pain, and found that we can predict, with great efficiency, who will respond to a placebo and who won't. It basically comes down to their respective brain anatomies and physiological characteristics. In subjects whose pain was aggravated by the placebo, the right side of the brain—responsible for emotions and reward—was larger. Also, based on survey results, these high responders exhibited higher levels of emotional alertness and greater pain tolerance. This is great for the patients, as by using inactive drugs instead of active ones, you can avoid side effects like addiction, and also effectively minimise the expense involved.

〉 Reflecting on your practice

1. Use the checklist below to decide what you did well and what you need to practise more. Set aside time to work on each area that you want to improve.

Highlight incorrect words checklist

I read the transcript and gained a general idea of the topic before listening.	○	I clicked on up to five or six words I believed to be incorrect.	○
I put my cursor at the beginning of the transcript just before the recording started.	○	I could easily tell which words were different between the transcript and the audio.	○
I followed the words in the transcript while listening.	○	I only selected words I was reasonably sure of – I didn't guess.	○

2. Check the answers in the Answer key. Were your answers correct? Try to think about how you could improve.

For more practice with *Highlight incorrect words* tasks, go to the **Online Question Bank**.

Go to the **Online Resources** for extra support with *Improving your Listening Skills*.

Write from dictation

Number of words in the sentence: around 10

Type of recording: audio only, single sentence

Number of these tasks in each test: 3–4

Time limit for all listening tasks: 45–57 minutes

Write from dictation tests how accurately you can re-construct a sentence you hear in written form, using your knowledge of grammar and vocabulary.

- You will hear a sentence.
- Then type the sentence exactly as you hear it.
- This task tests listening and writing skills.

1. The timer shows how much time is left for all the listening tasks in the test.
2. The audio status box will count down from seven seconds to zero, and then the audio will start.
3. While the recording is playing, you can type the sentence exactly as you hear it in the box. Or, you can write the sentence in your erasable booklet and then type it in the box afterwards.
4. You can edit text with the 'Cut', 'Copy' and 'Paste' buttons.
5. The 'Total Word Count' shows the number of words in your sentence.
6. Click 'Next' to go to the next question after you have checked your answer.

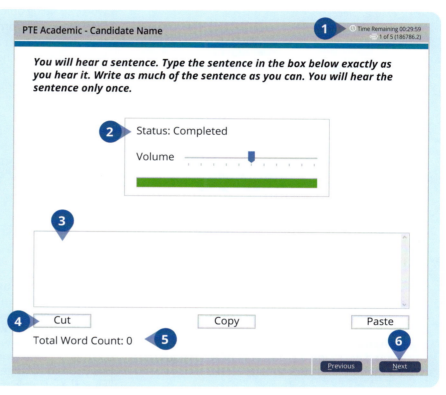

Skills tested

❯ Listening

- Understanding details
- Understanding grammar
- Comprehending concrete and abstract information
- Understanding academic vocabulary

❯ Writing

- Writing accurately from dictation
- Using accurate grammar, spelling and punctuation
- Using the correct vocabulary

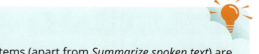

Points to remember: Listening tasks

- In listening tasks that also assess your writing, you will need to apply your listening skills in English and also think about what you write (relying on your vocabulary), and how you write it (using your knowledge of grammar, spelling and punctuation).

- Listening items (apart from *Summarize spoken text*) are not timed individually. **You will have between 45 to 57 minutes for all the listening items.** Make sure you practice managing your time effectively across all the tasks, to give yourself sufficient time to complete them.

WRITE FROM DICTATION | 119

Strategies for success › Before the test

Ensure that you are confident about spelling

1 Review the regular spelling conventions in English. Make a list of words you tend to find difficult to spell, especially words with *ie* or *ei* (e.g. *piece*, *receipt*), or double-consonant spellings like *mm*, *pp* and *ss* (e.g. *communication*, *disappointed, business*). Try to learn words with similar spelling together.

2 Be aware that a lot of words sound similar in English, but have very different spellings and sometimes, different meanings.

acccept	except
principal	principle
past	passed
piece	peace

3 Many words have different forms for different parts of speech e.g. *severity* (noun), *severe* (adjective), *severely* (adverb). In the test, you may mishear part of a word, so being able to work out which form of the word is correct and how to spell it can help you.

4 **Being able to guess the spelling of unfamiliar words is important.** Try writing down a small number of unfamiliar words you hear in online videos, academic podcasts and lectures. Choose important words that are related to the main theme of the text. Then check the spelling of these words (e.g. with a transcript of the recordings if available, or with a dictionary).

› Practice tips

You won't be able to remember the whole sentence so you will need to take notes of the main words while you listen. Practise listening to one-sentence extracts and **decide whether you prefer handwriting or typing** what you hear. Once you have made the decision, practice your chosen method and stick with it.

Native speakers of English don't pronounce every single word clearly. However, they do stress important words (usually nouns, verbs and adjectives) more clearly. **Practise identifying stressed words** in online lectures or podcasts. Pay attention to those words which are pronounced more clearly and see if you can build up a general picture of what the person is talking about.

Practice building up a sentence from stressed words. Listen to a short sentence from an online lecture or podcast. Play it two or three times. As you do so, write down the stressed words that you hear. Don't try to write down every single word. Then, without listening again, use the stressed words to create the full sentence. Use your knowledge of grammar and smaller words like *a*, *the*, *of* (which are not usually pronounced clearly) to construct the sentence. Then listen again to check your sentence.

Find transcripts of lectures or podcasts to work out the errors in your response. What kind of errors do you tend to make? Are they grammar, punctuation, or vocabulary based? Reflecting on what you write as you practice will help you pinpoint where you need to work on improving your skills.

Your score for this task

COMMUNICATIVE SKILLS
Listening ✔
Reading
Speaking
Writing ✔

ENABLING SKILLS
Grammar
Oral Fluency
Pronunciation
Spelling
Vocabulary
Written discourse

Look out!
You will get a score of zero if you:
- write nothing.
- write a sentence that's different from what you hear, e.g. one you memorised before the test.

› During the test

1 BEFORE LISTENING

Get ready before the audio status box reaches zero.
- If you are planning to type your notes place the cursor in the box so you are ready to start typing.
- If you are planning to take notes, have the erasable booklet and pen ready.

2 WHILE LISTENING

As soon as the recording starts, **begin taking notes** of what you hear.

Most importantly, **focus on meaning**. It's easier to remember meaning than details such as the grammar of the sentence.

Stick with either handwriting or typing, as you decided in your practice before the test. Write or type as quickly as you can.

Focus on the content words (nouns, verbs, adjectives and adverbs). These are usually stressed in the recording. You don't have to type or write the whole word now. You can use abbreviations (e.g. *dfclt* for *difficult*) and deal with spelling and the minor words (prepositions, articles) later.

3 AFTER LISTENING

Type the complete sentence into the response box.

Use your knowledge of grammar, spelling and vocabulary to **re-create anything you missed**, such as:
- small words (*are*, *be*, *to*, *a*, *the*, etc.)
- word endings (*-ed*, *-ment*, *-ing*, *-able*, etc.)
- plural endings
- punctuation

Keep an eye on the timer. These are the last tasks of the test, so don't spend too much time on one and leave not enough time for the others.

4 FINALLY

Re-read the sentence and **check the grammar, spelling, word forms and word order are correct**.

Make sure that you have **started with a capital letter** and **ended with a full stop**.

Re-read again and check for overall meaning.

Make sure you …

✔ **stick to the writing/typing method you have practised.**
  ✘ Don't change your method at the last minute.

✔ **finish note-taking before typing it in full.**
  ✘ Don't correct mistakes during the recording.

✔ **write what you hear.**
  ✘ Don't write a sentence you memorised before the test. You will score zero for doing this.

✔ **spell words correctly.**
  ✘ Don't worry about British or American spelling. Either form of spelling is OK for this task type. If you hear a sentence with *colour* in it, you will get the same score for the task whether you type 'color' or 'colour'.

✔ **pay attention to vocabulary and grammar.**
  ✘ Don't forget to check that your sentence makes sense both in meaning and grammatically.

 Watch the *Write from dictation: common mistakes* video for more tips and guidance on this task.

Practice › Write from dictation

Here is a sample *Write from dictation* task for you to practise.

 Practise *Write from dictation 2* here if you want to try *Write from dictation* without a time limit. Think about the strategies on pages 120–121. Then follow the task instructions.

 Find *Write from dictation 2* in the **Online Question Bank** resources to complete it under timed conditions.

> Write from dictation 2   **You will hear a sentence. Write the sentence in the box below exactly as you hear it. Write as much of the sentence as you can. You will hear the sentence only once.**
>
> _____
> _____

› Reflecting on your practice

1 Use the checklist below to decide what you did well and what you need to practise more. Set aside time to work on each area that you want to improve.

Write from dictation checklist

I was prepared to either type or write before the recording started.	○	I used my grammar, vocabulary and spelling knowledge to write the sentence.	○
I started writing as soon as the recording began.	○	I checked my sentence for meaning when I finished.	○
I focused on meaning while listening.	○	I checked my sentence for grammar, spelling and punctuation.	○

2 Check the answer in the Answer key. Was your answer correct? Try to think about how you could improve.

For more practice with *Write from dictation* tasks, go to the **Online Question Bank**.

Go to the **Online Resources** for extra support with *Improving your Listening Skills*.

Building confidence: Listening

› Effective listening skills

To achieve your test score goals, you may need to improve your general listening skills in English, which includes working on some of your enabling skills for listening (e.g. vocabulary, grammar and spelling).

LISTENING FOR STRUCTURE

Pay attention to how speech is structured. This can help you understand what you listen to.

Identify the specific context and topic quickly. Listen for the main topic or topics being covered and how they are related. Identifying the context of what you listen to, helps you focus on the topic, predict what they might talk about and the language they might use.

Understand common speaking structures. An opinion is likely to be followed by an explanation. A description of a problem is likely to be followed by a proposal for a solution. Recognising common patterns of speech can help you follow a speaker and anticipate what they are likely to say next.

Understand the logical development and sequence of what you hear. Look for and recognise key words, phrases or expressions that help to structure a speech or presentation. Listen for phrases that introduce, summarise or shift topics and indicate what the speaker is talking about and where they are leading (e.g. *first*, *finally* or *my last point is* …) or cohesive devices that link their ideas together (e.g. *so that*, *if … then …* or *consequently*). This kind of language can give you clues as to where the speaker will go next as well as the connections between ideas.

Listen for how the speaker groups ideas or information. This helps you understand which information is key and which gives general or supporting evidence. If you can learn to categorise information while you listen, you will be able to choose the key points to focus on in tasks such as *Re-tell lecture* or *Summarize spoken text*.

LISTENING FOR DETAIL OR SPECIFIC INFORMATION

Sometimes it is important to focus on listening for specific information to complete a task or use it for your own response.

Listen for key language. Train yourself to identify the most important details or facts in a presentation, argument or sequences of events. This can help you in tasks such as *Highlight correct summary*, *Fill in the blanks* and *Select missing word*, or to structure your response in *Summarize spoken text* tasks.

Use vocabulary you already know. Try to think about the language and phrases the speaker will use. This can help you guess what the speaker might say and is very useful for tasks such as *Select missing word* and *Multiple-choice, choose single answer* and *choose multiple answers* tasks. It will also mean you are more engaged with the subject and will be able to extract more meaning.

Expand your vocabulary knowledge to include useful academic vocabulary. When you listen to an academic lecture or presentation, you may hear unfamiliar words. Some words will be too subject-specific to be useful, but many are likely to reappear. Record any new words, phrases, synonyms, antonyms and collocations that might be useful.

Build your awareness of spoken grammar. Grammar can take on a slightly different form when spoken. For examples, contractions such as *could've* and *gonna* would never be written in academic texts but might still be spoken. They can change the meaning of sentences entirely so it's important to be aware of them.

Pay attention to pronunciation. Listing words that have similar pronunciation but different spellings (e.g. *affect/effect*, *except/accept*, *no/know*, *fair/fare*) can help you learn the differences and prepare for tasks such as *Write from dictation*.

LISTENING FOR OVERALL MEANING

Understanding the main message is often the most important part of any listening activity.

Listening for gist. It can be easy to get distracted during a long piece of spoken language, but it is important to concentrate in order to understand the topic, theme and overall message. Don't try to focus on every word or phrase that you hear. For example, in *Summarize spoken text* tasks, the important thing is conveying the gist of the speaker's message, rather than repeating it word for word.

Put the main points in your own words. Understanding the main points and being able to paraphrase them is a useful skill for tasks such as *Multiple-choice, choose multiple answers* tasks or any listening task where you need to summarise what the speaker says. Practise listening to short presentations and summarising the most important points from the talk in the simplest way possible. Show your summary to someone else: can they understand it? Do they agree that you have selected the main points?

Focus on understanding a speaker's attitude. You can do this by listening to the speaker and identifying how they use stress, tone and intonation to show feelings and opinions. It may tell you a lot about their opinion and how certain they are of it. For example, the way a speaker says words like *may*, *might* and *could* can change the idea they want to communicate. In *This may be a solution*, a speaker can indicate a high degree of uncertainty by stressing the word 'may' and saying it with a rising tone of voice.

 For more information and tips for improving listening skills, go to to **Improving Listening Skills** in the **Online Resources**

BUILDING CONFIDENCE: LISTENING

❯ Effective listening skills checklist

Think about your listening skills in English. Use this checklist to identify your strengths and areas where you could improve.

LISTENING FOR STRUCTURE

	I feel confident ✔	I could practise more ✔	I need to improve my skills ✔
I can identify whether I am listening for detail or for the gist of the topic and meaning.	●	●	●
I can follow the flow of ideas as I listen and see how they are similar or different.	●	●	●
I know how to separate key points from supporting ideas or information.	●	●	●
I can identify key words and expressions that the speaker uses to structure their speech.	●	●	●
I can recognise signposting words that highlight the speaker's purpose.	●	●	●

LISTENING FOR DETAIL OR SPECIFIC INFORMATION

	I feel confident ✔	I could practise more ✔	I need to improve my skills ✔
I can understand key words or phrases about specific academic information.	●	●	●
I can identify gaps in what I understand and use the context of the topic to fill in the details.	●	●	●
I understand what paraphrasing is and when a speaker might be paraphrasing.	●	●	●
I have knowledge of how words can have similar sounds and pronunciation, but different spellings and meanings.	●	●	●
I can put good punctuation and spelling techniques into practice to write down what I hear accurately.	●	●	●
I can use good grammar techniques to write down what I hear accurately.	●	●	●
I have solid knowledge of grammar to help me understand how a speaker phrases their ideas.	●	●	●

LISTENING FLUENCY

	I feel confident ✔	I could practise more ✔	I need to improve my skills ✔
I can understand the gist when listening without understanding every word.	●	●	●
I can recognise key words or phrases which provide clues to the topic or the gist.	●	●	●
I can understand the speaker's point of view and attitude by locating and understanding relevant words and phrases.	●	●	●
I can identify how the speaker uses stress and tone to express their feelings about the topic.	●	●	●
I can interpret a speaker's intonation as I listen to get clues about when new points might be coming.	●	●	●
I can locate enough relevant information and general meaning when listening to form a response or make a confident choice of answer.	●	●	●
I can ensure my written summary contains the relevant key information and supporting details.	●	●	●

124 | EFFECTIVE LISTENING CHECKLIST

› **Building blocks for test confidence**

1 **READING SKILLS FOR LISTENING**
Improving your general reading skills can help you prepare for listening tasks, as this will help you to:
- Prepare for what you hear in order to construct an appropriate response;
- Locate supporting points or examples in a text to help you listen for detail;
- Find the most accurate summary to describe what you hear;
- Understand academic vocabulary and guess unfamiliar words;
- Understand information which is not described directly;
- Match written information to information you listen to;
- Balance thinking about what you read while you listen.

2 **WRITING SKILLS FOR LISTENING**
Improving your general writing skills will also help you to:
- Communicate the main points of a lecture;
- Organise ideas in a logical way;
- Use words and phrases appropriate to the context;
- Use accurate grammar, spelling and punctuation;
- Match similar meanings in written text to speech, even when they are formulated differently;
- Write accurately from dictation.

3 **NOTETAKING**
Write brief notes while listening if you are concerned you might forget something important. This is necessary in PTE Academic listening tasks. Your notes will help you to remember and use the information you have heard. Before the test, develop a notetaking technique you feel comfortable using on test day, one that helps you to take notes quickly.

Abbreviations can be helpful for taking notes during listening tasks, as you have little time to write full words or expressions.

4 **CRITICAL THINKING SKILLS**
Critical thinking skills are essential whenever you listen to someone speak. Your ability to question, compare and analyse ideas will mean that you are an active listener. To improve your critical thinking while listening, practise skills such as analysing information you hear and reflecting on what a speaker says or implies.

5 **TIME MANAGEMENT**
You have to make sure you are managing your time correctly throughout the whole listening section. It is easy to spend too long on one activity. Equally, if you work too quickly, you might make unnecessary errors. Try completing a practice test under timed conditions. Use the chart on page XXX and practise spending a suitable amount of time on each task.

› **Keys for confidence**

Practise listening with background noise. Other test takers in the same room may be speaking when you are trying to listen. Also, because PTE Academic uses authentic sources, there may also be background noise or other distracting effects within the audio tracks themselves. Practise listening to English recordings in busy places and blocking out background noise.

Listen to English as much as you can. Keep your brain tuned into English at all times as you prepare for the test. Find series, documentaries, podcasts, etc. that you enjoy and want to listen to regularly. Listen to different accents and a wide range of recordings and videos.

Glossary

abbreviation (n): a short form of a word (e.g. _Dr_ = _doctor_)

ability (n): the skill or power that you need to do something

abstract (adj): a general idea or feeling (e.g. truth, beauty); not something you can touch

accent (n): the way someone speaks that shows where they are from (e.g. _a British accent, a New York accent_)

accurate (adj): correct and true

antonym (n): a word which has the opposite meaning to another word (e.g. _big – small_)

appropriate (adj): when something is correct or OK in one situation (the opposite is _inappropriate_, when something is wrong for a situation)

argue (v): to try and explain (using reasons and examples) why something is true

attitude (n): the opinions and feelings you have about something

categorise (v): to sort things into groups, according to what type of things they are (see also _classify_)

chronological (adj): when something is _in chronological order_, it is arranged according to when things happened in time

classify (v): to sort things into groups, according to what type of things they are (see also _categorise_)

collocation (n): words which are often found or used together (e.g. _make a decision, pay attention to someone_)

cohesion (n): if there is cohesion in a text, then the information is connected and things relate to other things to create one clear, logical text (not just a group of unconnected sentences)

cohesive devices (n): the things we use these to create cohesion in a text, including linking words and phrases (_however, for example_, etc.), pronouns (_he, our_, etc.), reference words (_this, those_, etc.) and so on

complex idea (n): an idea which has many things to think about and may be difficult to understand

comprehend (v): to understand

concrete (adj): information that is clear and certain

conjunction (n): a word such as _and, but, or, while_ which connects information in one sentence

connotation (n): the special meaning of a word that makes it different from other words which are similar (e.g. _slim_ has a positive connotation, _skinny_ has a negative connotation)

context (n): the situation something appears or exists in

counter-argument (n): an argument against another argument (see also _opposing argument_)

criticise (v): to say or argue that something is not correct or not good enough

cursor (n): a shape that you can move around a computer screen to show where you are working

definition (n): something that explains the meaning of a word or an idea

denotation (n): the main meaning of a word

distract (v): to make it difficult for someone to focus on or think about something

disturb (v): to interrupt someone so that they cannot continue what they were doing

eliminate (v): to remove something, because it isn't needed

evaluate (v): to decide how important or good something is

evidence (n): the information you have which shows that something is (or isn't) true

exaggerate (v): to make something sound better, bigger, worse, etc. than it really is

explicit (adj): information that is clear and direct

feature (n): a part of something that is important or special

flow (n): when something moves or continues smoothly and clearly

fluency (n): the ability to speak in a smooth, confident way without stopping or repeating yourself

gist (n): the main idea

implication (n): something that is communicated, but not directly

implicit (adj): information that is not communicated directly

imply (v): to communicate an idea without saying it directly

individually (adj): separately or alone (not in a group or with others)

infer (v): to guess or decide what someone is saying

inference (n): a guess or decision you make about what someone is saying

inform (v): to give information

instinct (n): what you use to make a guess about something, using your feelings, but not really thinking about it

intonation (n): the way your voice changes (e.g. by going up or down) to add meaning to what you're saying

linking (n): the way some words are linked together as one sound (e.g. _the_apple_) when we're speaking quickly and naturally

linking phrase (n):	a phrase that connects information in one sentence (or part of a sentence) to another (e.g. *for example, that's why*, etc.)
linking word (n):	a word that connects information in one sentence (or part of a sentence) to another (e.g. *although, because, however*, etc.)
logical (adj):	something that is sensible and clear
reconstruct (v):	to collect information and make a complete copy of something
main idea (n):	the most important idea
memorise (v):	to learn words, information, etc. so that you can remember them later
nominalisation (n):	when verbs or other words are turned into nouns (e.g. *Please* decide *...* → *Please make a* decision *...*)
opposing argument (n):	an argument against another argument (see also *counter-argument*)
organise (v):	to arrange a text so that the ideas are clear and make sense
overall meaning (n):	the general meaning of a whole text (not just one part of it)
paraphrase (v):	to say or write something in a shorter or different way
penalty (n):	a punishment (e.g. getting a lower score) for doing something wrong
persuade (v):	to try and make someone think or feel or do something
prefix (n):	a group of letters which is added to the front of a word to make a new word (e.g. <u>un</u>important, <u>dis</u>appear)
preposition (n):	a word that is used with another noun to talk about place, time, direction, etc. (e.g. <u>at</u> 5 o'clock, <u>on</u> the internet, <u>around</u> the world)
proficient (adj):	being very good at something
purpose (n):	the reason you do something
relationship (n):	the way that two or more things (e.g. ideas) are connected
relevant (adj):	when something is connected to, or relates to, what is happening or being discussed (the opposite is *irrelevant*, when something is not useful or related to a situation)
rhythm (n):	a regular, repeated pattern of sounds
scan (v):	to read something quickly to find the information that you want
sense group (n):	a group of words which are linked together to make one piece of information (e.g. *an increasing number of people*)
signalling word (n):	a word or phrase that helps the listener or reader understand what is coming next (e.g. *The most important thing is ..., In addition, ...*, etc.)
skim (v):	to read something quickly so that you can understand the main ideas (not the details)
specific (adj):	one particular thing or person
structure (n & v):	the way the parts of something (e.g. a text) are connected and made to create a whole
summarise (v):	to give the main information in a short way
supporting detail (n):	information which helps to make an argument stronger, e.g. by adding an example, a reason or an explanation
symbol (n):	a picture or shape that has a meaning (e.g. @ & √ etc.)
tress (n):	the way we say a word (or part of a word) more loudly or clearly than others
subordinate clause (n):	part of a sentence which adds information, but cannot exist on its own (e.g. *Many people cannot concentrate <u>when they are stressed</u>.*)
suffix (n):	a group of letters which is added to the end of a word to make a new word (e.g. *slow<u>ly</u>, use<u>ful</u>*)
syllable (n):	a word or a part of a word which has one vowel sound (e.g. the word *in.for.ma.tion* has four syllables)
synonym (n):	a word which has a similar meaning to another word (e.g. *big – large*)
technical (adj):	technical words are words used by specific groups of people (e.g. scientists, engineers, etc.) and may not be easy for other groups of people to understand
thesaurus (n):	a type of dictionary showing words with similar meanings
tone (of voice) (n):	the way your voice sounds, which shows how you feel about something
topic sentence (n):	a sentence in a paragraph (often, but not always the first sentence) which summarises what the paragraph will focus on
transcript (n):	a written version of something that someone says
under timed conditions (phr):	to do something in a number of minutes or hours
unfamiliar (adj):	something that you don't know about or haven't seen before
weak forms (n):	the way some words sound shorter or less clear when we're speaking quickly and naturally in English
written discourse (n):	written communication (e.g. an article, a story, a report)
visualise (v):	to make a picture of something in your mind

GLOSSARY | 127

Pearson Education Limited
KAO Two
KAO Park
Hockham Way
Harlow, Essex
CM17 9SR
England
and Associated Companies throughout the world.

english.com/pteacademicguide

© Pearson Education Limited 2020

All rights reserved; no part of this publication may be reproduced, stored in a retrieval system, or transmitted in any form or by any means, electronic, mechanical, photocopying, recording, or otherwise without the prior written permission of the Publishers

First published 2010, 2012

ISBN: 978-1-292-34198-9

Set in Open Sans 9/12pt
Prined in Slovakia by Neografia

Author Acknowledgements
David Hill with Anushka Fowler
(The Education Craftworks Pty Ltd)
Simon Cotterill

Acknowledgements
The publishers and author(s) would like to thank the following people and institutions for their feedback and comments during the development of the material:

Abdulkadir Gullu (Turkey), Cahit Taylan (Turkey), Connie Baques (Vietnam), Dr Swamy Mavsnarayana (India), Jurine Ruperto (Philippines), Louise Fitzgerald (Australia), Müge Akgedik (Turkey), Mümin Şen (Turkey), Neslihan Atcan Altan (Turkey), Sinem Unlu (Turkey), Tarik Younes Guernane (UK), Suzanne Beckerley (Turkey), Cheah Swi Ee (Malaysia), Richard Swanson (New Zealand), and Martha Xia (Australia).

Photo acknowledgements
123RF/MichaelSpring P.40; Shutterstock/vovan P.50
All other images © Pearson Education

Illustrations acknowledgements
Designers Educational 7, 11, 13, 18, 22, 23, 26, 30, 34, 36, 38, 42, 52, 56, 66, 70, 74, 92, 96, 100, 104, 108, 112, 116;
Pen & Ink 33